Wishing you success in life and business

More Leads More Clients

by

Leon Streete

MORE LEADS MORE CLIENTS

The10 Step Marketing Manifesto To Becoming One of the Most Valued and Highly Paid Coaches in Your Industry

First Edition for Print November 2018

ISBN: 978-1-64467-682-0 paperback
ISBN: 978-1-64467-681-3 eBook

Editor: Christy Rutherford
Cover Design: Vikiana
Illustrations: Viral Bhavsar

Praise For

More Leads More Clients

Leon has written the no nonsense book about marketing and sales generation. This book has literally hundreds of golden nuggets that you can take away and apply in your business. The key here is that you have to take action and his chapter summaries, case studies and stories make the job that much easier. If you want more Leads more Clients this is one of the books that should be on your book shelf.

Dr Karl George MBE
Director Governance Forum Ltd, karlgeorge.com

If you allow it to… this book could change your business. Packed with easy to apply nuggets that can have an instant impact on your business growth, Leon brings it home. Video sales letters - have worked for me! What's measured gets improved - has worked for me! And… I loved the "what to do when your client says no!"
Read and APPLY this now.

David Hyner
Professional Speaker, davidhyner.com

I'm grateful to have read an advance copy of Leon Streete's new book, More Leads, More Clients. It's action packed with tangible marketing strategies that will grow your income and help more people. I often get a lot of books sent to me and many of them are full of fluff. This book is legit, and well worth your investment of time and money.

AJ Mihrzad
#1 Best Selling Author, Founder of OnlineSupercoach.com

I have been a huge fan of Leon Streete's work since I first met him in 2015. With his book More Leads More Clients, Leon continues his legacy of helping coaches and small business owners understand and master proven and personalized strategies for attracting great clients so they can have the impact they're here to have. A practical and useful read.

Eleanor Beaton

Host, Fierce Feminine Leadership:
The Success Podcast for Ambitious Women
eleanorbeaton.com

What a gem! 'More Leads More Clients' cuts to the truth of how to generate more business in less time, utilising known and tested principles and strategies. Author, Leon Streete, distinguishes himself because I personally know he has engaged these ideas to hugely improve his results. Critically, the principles he teaches work. I have used many of them to consistently generate multiple 6 and 7 figure incomes annually. I just love 'Pitching Yourself to People' and the chapter 'action summaries'.

Derek Mills

Author – 'The 10-Second Philosophy®', Executive Producer of 'Think and Grow Rich' the movie, Founder of DailyStandards.com

Leon's book gives you the exact blueprint needed to get more leads and convert them into high paying clients. He broke down complex systems and created easily implementable plans to get the results you desire. The illustrations further simplify what took me years to learn and figure out. If you're ready to get paid doing what you love, get this book!

Christy Rutherford

6x Number #1 Best Selling Author, Women's Career Success Coach

I've been anticipating this book for a long time. As someone who teaches about the importance of having a systems driven business, to now have access to Leon's proven lead generation system, laid out in this easy to follow and actionable book is GOLD. Leon doesn't just write about this stuff, it's what he does. If you want results, then you need to read this book, and implement the principals taught within it.

Tony L Brown

Author – Standard Procedure. Process Consultant at TonylBrown.com

Dedication

To Magdalena your love and belief in me writing this book is a big part of the reason why I completed it. Having great success with your own book gave me the inspiration needed to complete this milestone, thank you my Kochanie – I love you.

Reuben and Renae, my children, thank you for filling my heart with love everyday and giving me with the responsibility to lead and show you what's possible. You inspire me to constantly improve in order to provide you both with the best I have to offer as a father.

Contents

Foreword

"One doesn't always find shortcuts to success. But at least in this instance, for those coaches who need marketing knowhow to succeed in their career, this book provides a path."

by Chad E Cooper

IF YOU ARE A COACH or aspiring to become one, you know you are in a crowded field. This is the reality whether you are focusing on business, executive or leadership coaching, life, relationship or career coaching or on any other specialized area.

Your success as a coach does not depend entirely on you. The person you are coaching holds the reigns to their ultimate success or failure. For this reason, most effective coaches, like Leon Streete, cannot merely be measured on their talents alone. They are measured, in the long run, by the results they produce working with their clients.

Leon Streete is a coach specializing in the marketing niche. Over the years, with hard work, integrity, dedication and commitment to his work, and to those who seek his services, Leon has produced results. He is called "The Lead Generation Coach" because he produces great results for his clients in his chosen field of marketing and lead generation.

Success of a coach is all about results. Going through *More Leads More Clients: The 10 Step Marketing Manifesto To Becoming One of the Most Valued and Highly Paid Coaches In Your Industry*, I am certain this book too will produce results for each coach and aspiring coach who decides to take its content to heart.

The book will produce results for those who have been lucky to come in one on one contact with Leon or in a group session and get the benefit of mining his treasure trove of marketing and coaching experience first-hand. The same goes for his numerous followers on his podcasts, which won the award of "UK's Best Business Podcast", for interviewing successful entrepreneurs and experts.

With this book, his first, Leon Streete goes one step further. For those who have not encountered him, but, aspire to become a successful coach in their chosen field whether they are just starting out or seeking ways to more effectively market their own services, this book is going to provide step by step guidance towards successfully marketing their coaching practice. They should consider this book — *More Leads More Clients* — their 24/7 reference and guide towards realizing their dream of coaching success.

Speaking for myself, despite the successes I've achieved in my coaching career, marketing is not my thing. I'd rather have a coaching session with someone over coffee than spend my time doing a podcast to market myself. Coaching is my strength. Marketing is not. It is something I'd rather not have to do.

The reality though, is that all those who are intent on achieving coaching success need to market themselves. We are all forced into engaging in marketing activities to promote our services whether we like them or not.

Leon Streete is different. He finds marketing and lead generation easy and he does an excellent job of it; for himself and for his clients. And he produces excellent results for those who seek his coaching services. In this, he's eminently qualified to write this book.

I know there are so many coaches, who like me, would rather not have to do any marketing at all. They'd rather coach people than be blowing their own trumpet. But in a competitive and crowded field like coaching, regardless of your specialty or niche, or how excellent you are as a coach, marketing is imperative to success. You cannot simply become a valued and highly paid coach without effectively marketing your services. And for most coaches, engaging the services of outside marketing experts or consultants may not be a viable option. This is especially so at the beginning of their coaching career.

For those who'd rather spend most of their time coaching—no one can afford to neglect marketing altogether—Leon Streete offers an excellent solution through *More Leads More Clients.* Whether you love or hate marketing, follow Leon's *10 Step Marketing Manifesto* and you are assured of marketing success.

One doesn't always find shortcuts to success. But at least in this instance, for those coaches who need marketing knowhow to succeed in their career, this book provides a path.

Without more leads, and more clients, you have no way of proving that you have what it takes to produce results as a coach and guide people who count on you towards success. Without more clients, how can you build a reputation for yourself as an effective coach? You cannot. This is why *More Leads More Clients: The 10 Step Marketing Manifesto To Becoming One of the Most Valued and Highly Paid Coaches In Your Industry* is an essential resource for every coach.

I recommend reading the book from the beginning to the end. Then, on and off, refer to it as you develop and implement your marketing measures. However smart you are, it is impossible to simply absorb all the nuggets that Leon Streete has imparted in this book in one go. Especially if you've never tried to market your coaching services, some aspects will become clear to you only from experience, of failures and substandard results.

The value of *The 10 Step Marketing Manifesto* lies in its ability to reignite that spark of an idea as you browse through the book for the umpteenth time; and not always when you are seeking definitive answers to a marketing conundrum.

In parting, I say: Believe in yourself. Believe in your own ability to improve the lives of those you coach for the better. Believe in your dream of becoming one of the most valued and highly paid coaches in your industry. And then, use the lessons that Leon Streete imparts in *The 10 Step Marketing Manifesto To Becoming One of the Most Valued and Highly Paid Coaches In Your Industry".*

I wish you all the best in both marketing and coaching success!

Chad E Cooper
Legendary Lifestyle® Coach
www.chadecooper.com

Acknowledgements

THERE ARE MANY PEOPLE WHO helped to make this book possible and deserve my appreciation.

Robert Dene Smith and Phil Faulkner, our 18 months of partnership in business helped forge ideas, concepts and insights to making what I do an adventure of learning, failure and success. These are blessings that I can now take forward to help others.

David Hyner, a friend who demonstrates integrity, resilience and faith. You remind me to "go rhino" and smash through my goals.

Todd Brown, coming across your work and mastermind events helped me gain a more strategic approach to marketing. You learned from the best and I am grateful to receive the knowledge you passed on.

Derek Mills, the lasting effects of your teachings on my life have become a place of awareness in knowing that I can change my future within 10 seconds.

Julie Anne Eason thanks for inspiring me to lay down my thoughts into a book. Your work has helped me realise that what I have in my heart and head need to be shared with the world.

Tony Brown, thank you for being an inspiration from our days of dj'ing and producing music, to doing what you do in your adventures as a multiple business owner - Thank you.

Christy Rutherford thank you for taking my marketing brain dump and helping me edit and turn this into something worthy of my efforts. You truly are a Leadership Coach, friend, and kick-ass accountability multi-best-selling Book Boss!

My clients and supporters, without you this book would not be possible. You have provided emotions, ideas, thoughts, tears and happiness. I've had to think bigger and constantly evolve to be better than I was yesterday, to provide you with the best of who I am today – Thank you.

"Together We Rise…"

Who This Book Is For

This book is for you if... You're either thinking about setting up a coaching business or you're already established and knee-deep looking for answers to help grow what you've already started. It's also for you if:

1. You wish to increase sales and have a system for generating continuous leads.

2. You wish to save time and money when running your marketing campaigns.

3. You want insider knowledge into the strategies of how to boost your marketing efforts.

4. You get lost in the technical language and want to make marketing work for your business.

5. You actually have a budget for marketing and time to invest, with the intention of getting the best results and scaling your business.

Getting Started…

How this book is structured

THIS BOOK HAS BEEN STRUCTURED to maximise where you are in your business so that you have the best possible blueprint to follow.

I suggest reading the book several times to get the most out of the insight offered. The first time, read the book from start to finish with minimal highlighting. Get a feel for the content and determine if it resonates with you. Are there nuggets of information, techniques or ideas you can use in your own business?

Then, read it again and do the following to get the best results from the insight offered.

- Read with a purpose. Key in on the goals you want to achieve.
- Highlight the information, statements and content that speak to where you are right now in your business. Take notes on the side of the pages.
- Visualise how the content relates to your business.
- ***Document what you learn.*** Whether you use a notepad, journal or Word / PowerPoint document. Write down the action steps that will impact your business and keep it close to you for continual reference. For me, this is the most powerful way to improve the systems and procedures of my business. Transferring the author's knowledge to mine.

Make highlights throughout this book use it as an active reference tool, transfer the knowledge into your business and work it like a well-oiled machine that fuels your passion in business and prints you money as your reward.

FREE Workbook

As part of this book, be sure to download the accompanying workbook. I've designed it to allow you to action the key points I raise throughout the book and to ensure you get the most out of the teaching, lessons and principles I explain for you and your business.

Simply access the workbook plus additional resources, interviews, PDF guides, training videos and more for free here:
www.moreleadsmoreclientsbook.com/resources

The 10 Steps of Marketing Success

TO BE PART OF THE "More Leads More Clients Movement", follow the 10 steps that are laid out below for you to follow. Each step is tied to a chapter of this book, so as you read and take action, you move closer to the next level in your journey.

- **Step1: Strategy** – Create a goal bigger than who you are now, and with time and continued work, you will grow into the person to make it happen. Let patience be your virtue.

- **Step 2: Positioning** – Life and how you're viewed is all about perspective. So position yourself to be viewed as the best possible version of yourself. Bring people with you, educate them, inspire them and set them free.

- **Step 3: Direct Marketing** – Create hooks that grab your prospects imagination

- **Step 4: Products & Services** – Create wow experiences that provide transformation, fun, and happiness

- **Step 5: Autonomy** – Do more with less effort. Systemise the routine and humanise the exception (where initiative and creativity is needed)

- **Step 6: Tactics** – Find the places where your customers hang out and engage them.

- **Step 7: Convert** – Create methods for getting more sales.

- **Step 8: Selling** – Create an environment where you help your customers get what they want with your products. When you It's only when you sell that clients get value, and value is only determined by the client. Without sales, you have no clients, without clients – you have no business.

- **Step 9: Growth** – All growth comes from persistent action centered around a positive TEAM.

- **Step 10: Secret Weapon** – Your ability to move forward regardless if you have undesired results for a moment. Keep your dream in front of you and share your gifts. Make Success Your Duty and act on it with passion and determination.

Let's do this!

CREATE YOUR MARKETING PLAN

MESSAGE TOPICS

CONTENT STYLES

TIME PLAN

RESPONSIBILITIES

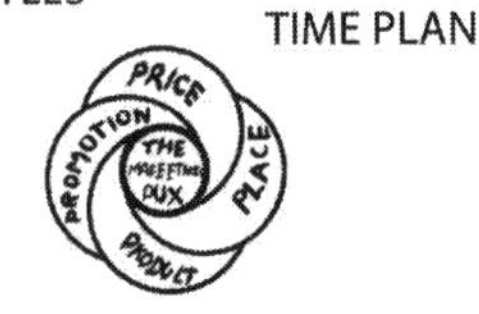

THE MARKETING MIX (TACTICS)

CHAPTER 1

How To Create a Winning Marketing Strategy

Great and profitable Coaches, Consultants and Business Owners continually look for techniques to improve their Marketing and Sales because they know there's another level. I'm here to share there are countless ways to become successful when launching and growing your business. You can grow it to exceed the levels you've envisioned in your hopes, dreams and desire.

With the advancement of technology in the past decade, there have been significant shifts in the methods your message is delivered to your audience. There are new ways to target your desired customers. Different variations to keep their attention. We're now in a fast-paced environment as new features and the culture of the early technology adopters "bell curve" continue to sway back and forth between competitors and market forces.

These "new and improved" methods are no more than tactics and can change in an instant. There have been updates in technology, such as Google's Algorithm, where you can see your website results rise or disappear from a key position in the search results. Facebook is known to constantly change its News Feed Algorithm and has the ability to significantly reduce the reach of your posts.

To remain competitive and relevant, you have to adapt to the unexpected changes of these giant marketing and advertising platforms, whilst focusing on the key to having success in your business, which includes learning how to serve the needs of your customer or fix their problems.

Problems, Challenges and Opportunities

In the book, *Ready Fire Aim*, by Michael Masterson, he shares the four stages of a business: Infancy, Childhood, Adolescence and Adulthood.

As a business owner under the $1 million mark, you're in *Infancy*. Since you don't know what you're doing, which is your main problem, your main challenge is selling. The opportunity you need to create is achieving minimum critical numbers. The additional skill you need is getting the business going and selling.

At $1 – $10 million, you're in *Childhood*. Breaking even or losing money is your main problem. Your main challenge is creating additional profitable products quickly. Your main opportunity is becoming a business of innovation increasing cash flow and becoming profitable. The additional skill needed is coming up with a constant stream of new tipping point ideas.

At $10 – $50 million you're in *Adolescence* and at $50 – $300 million you're in *Adulthood*. In these stages, marketing and sales are no longer your biggest challenges, it's managing the operation.

The key to all of this information offered is understanding that strategy must come before tactics. Strategy is long term. It's the goal that becomes a blueprint of how your customer must be won. Strategy is not the direct outreach (tactics) to get your customer.

When you apply this insight, you'll be on the right path and stop wasting time. You'll also have less pain and frustration with your business. Understanding Marketing Strategy will get you in alignment with where you need to be.

Get Your A-Team

What is a marketing strategy?

"An organization's strategy that combines all of its marketing goals into one comprehensive plan. A good marketing strategy should be drawn from market research and focus on the right product mix in order to achieve the maximum profit potential and sustain the business. The marketing strategy is the foundation of a marketing plan." *Businessdictionary.com*

The key element in the definition above is, "the foundation of a marketing plan..." With a good marketing plan, you can take an idea and bring it to life or take a dream and make it reality. Many coaches skip this part because they think a marketing strategy is a comprehensive bound or stapled document because of its complexity, they find it too daunting to even start or finish.

The need for a strategic approach was epitomised in a tv programme I watched in the 1980's. More importantly, they always showed the need to have a plan that needed to be adaptable and fluid like water.

I'm sure you're wondering what that programme was. Let me share...

> "In 1972, a crack commando unit was sent to prison by a military court for a crime they didn't commit. These men promptly escaped from a maximum security stockade to the Los Angeles underground. Today, still wanted by the government, they survive as soldiers of fortune. If you have a problem if no one else can help and if you can find them....maybe you can hire The A-Team."
> *The A-Team - "Opening Monologue"*

If we relate this to you right now, in each episode of the A-Team, they were faced with helping someone (your prospects) who was in distress (had a problem), and was typically being picked on by some *bad guys* (market forces and other challenges).

The A-Team was contacted by phone, which would somehow be from a referral or they would come across them coincidentally (your marketing campaigns). Upon speaking to the person in trouble, the A-Team would choose to help (after qualifying them).

Then they would devise a strategy (a marketing strategy) that included research by scoping out what the bad guys were up to and documenting this behaviour (market research), after enough evidence had been gathered, they would implement their plan by creating a solution or weapon (your product or service) that would stop the bad guys and finally allow the victim to live happy and free (completing the cycle of another happy customer served).

At the conclusion of each episode, they would say, "We love it when a plan comes together."

This programme taught me a critical lesson. That a solid plan would get you the desired result or as Hollywood would say, "A happy ending."

However, in the real world, sometimes things go bad, and you don't always get the positive result you hoped to achieve. Sometimes you will fail, but remember failure is temporary, so don't dwell on it for long periods of times. It's a part of the process of building your muscle to be able to sustain a successful business.

Necessary Elements of Your Marketing Strategy

Your marketing strategy outlines your desired objectives and *WHAT* you need to achieve with your marketing. It is largely shaped by your business goals.

It should include:

- The service or product you provide
- The long-term goals of your marketing plan
- An analysis of your consumers, including demographics and buying patterns (recency, frequency & unit of sale)
- Research (market & competitors)

You may have one or many goals within your strategy. They may include:

- Increase sales or set a sales target
- Acquire (quantity) new customers
- Increase repeat buying with existing customers
- Offer existing customers exclusive offers
- Retain existing profitable customers
- Make customers feel more valued
- Improve customer loyalty
- Introduce a new product or service
- Increase your market share
- Establish a better brand presence
- Launch an advertising campaign
- Launch a PR campaign
- Encourage word of mouth referrals
- Ensure your business stays current, relevant and widespread

The Exact Steps to Create Your Strategy

By now, you should have a clear understanding of the goals that you want to achieve in your business. This is a list of key areas to include in your marketing strategy as you should align them with your desired outcomes and goals. The key areas to include are:

1. **Market Research** – Conducting extensive research on your target audience, their preferences, desires, willingness to pay, etc. Also, a detailed list of your competitors and what they're doing to achieve great results.
2. **Market & Niche** – Choosing a market where prospects are already buying and determining the overall market size. Then look for ways to carve your own niche to capture a percentage of the market.

3. **Financial Goal** – Sales revenue. Detail the desired number of customers or profit in a specified period of time. Monthly, quarterly, annually and long-term goals.
4. **Product** – Defining your product or service
   - **Four P's –** Product, Placement, Pricing & Packaging
5. **Message** – Defining your unique selling proposition. The key here is not to do what everyone else is doing. Your need to stand out and your message needs to be unique.
6. **SWOT** – Analyse your current standing and market. Strengths, Weaknesses, Opportunities, and Threats.
7. **Executive Summary** –Should be a short summary of the items listed in steps 1-6. It will provide a macro level summary of marketing plan. I should not be too detailed or in the weeds. A broad overview of the overall plan.

How To Read Your Prospects Mind

When it comes to market research, I know for many of you, me included at one point (when I was losing learning in business) this may at first be a case of here we go "boring". But figuring out who your audience is and where they hangout is crucial to understanding them. It's very difficult to find something or someone if you don't know what you're actually looking for.

Properly conducted, market research will give you the ability to put your business in front of your target audience and make them feel like you read their mind. They'll say, "How did he/she know that's what I'm experiencing..."

There are two types of information to consider in your market research.

1. Specific: competitors, products, other people's marketing
2. General: any place, current events, history

Your research must help you identify the location of your hot market and target audience. Where do they hang out? What books or films have they read? Which gurus or influencers do they follow?

You can find valuable information (1) Online (Internet) and (2) Offline (Phone &In Person)

Online

Google Keyword Planner – The leading search engine that allows you to research keywords and phrases that are searched by consumers each month. It gives you the size of the demand for the searches that align with your service or product offering for your customers.

Clickbank – An online marketplace and top 100 internet retailer. Clickbank is a leader in digital e-commerce, driving over $3 Billion in sales, serving over 200 Million customers and working with more than 6 million entrepreneurs (course/product creators) in 190 countries around the world.

Facebook Audience Insights – With the biggest social media membership of over 2.1 billion people (in 2018), Facebook is the leader of customer insight data. The site allows you to create lists of people who you can target based on interests and demographics of over 300+ options – Mind blowing!

Forums – An Internet forum, or message board, is an online discussion website where people can hold conversations in the form of posted messages. Generally, there are forums for different niches and the more you research, the more you'll discover. Most people are familiar with Groups found on Facebook and LinkedIn, which are essentially the newer equivalent of forums.

SRDS Lists – These lists are supplied by list brokers. People who have extensive lists of customers in different markets who have bought opted in and generally received, purchased or communicated an interest in an offer by phone or post. Post or direct mail still works and converts.

You buy lists in bundles of 1000, known as (M). So, for each M you buy you will pay X amount. For instance, 3 times M may cost you £150 etc.

The great thing about these lists is that you're investing in a list of people who have bought before. This is key information to have because if they've bought already, it simply comes down to you convincing them with the right persuasion to buy your product too.

In order to pick the right list for your needs, there are three things to consider. Consider the following: recency, frequency, and unit of sale.

1. **Recency** -How recent was the purchase of someone who bought something similar to what you're selling. The more recent, the more receptive they will be buying from you.
2. **Frequency**- How often someone bought a particular item. This increases their desire for a similar type of service or product.
3. **Unit of sale**- The price of the product that a person recently bought. The price gives you an indicator of their willingness to pay and if your price point aligns with that.

Amazon – Using this platform as a research tool, can be very handy in a number of key areas. Going through the different book categories and sub categories leads you to the hidden gem of information Amazon highlights. It also shows different niches that are profitable based on the books that are sold and in high demand. This is valuable insight when it comes to targeting your audience. For example:

1. *Best Selling Books* – You can determine the trending topics within a niche. These are products your potential customers have purchased.
2. *Competitors and Partners* – Research the authors; check their websites, products and content they're putting out in addition to the books. Maybe they are key authorities within your chosen sub market that can lead to partnerships, interviews, JVs or simply insight into what they've done already that you haven't considered.

3. *Reviews* – Read the reviews and pay attention to positive and negative comments. Positive reviews affirm what they liked, and the negative reviews may offer you insights into what is missing and what your audience need or still have a problem with.
4. *Related Products & Upsells* – On the product page descriptions, pay attention to "Frequently Bought Together" and "Look For Similar Items By Category." These products can add to your content and product ideas. Use this market data to gain a greater understanding of your target audience.

YouTube: Research YouTube and see what's already in your market. There's a lot of information and in many cases it can result in information overload and distractions. Assembling a playlist of relevant videos will allow you to see videos that offer great value relevant to your audience.

Podcasts – Another great starting point to see and hear what your competitors are up to, are podcasts on iTunes and Stitcher Radio. Podcasts give you the opportunity to analyse how hosts engage their audience (in their episode content and the website and landing pages etc).

How they get involved in the podcast providers community through other social channels, such as Facebook/LinkedIn groups, forum or private paid memberships, etc. The insight gathered from your research findings will allow you to build a strong, powerful and persuasive campaign that speaks to what your audience desires and is willing to pay for.

Competitors – There are only a few rare, unique people in any market. Don't kid yourself into believing that no one exists in the market like you because "you are unique." Be open and think what your customers may consider as an alternative to your services. If you don't have any competitors, you may find that instead of your customers choosing you, they may not act at all.

Consider this – while you're online scrolling through social media timelines, what are they displaying in the corners of the page? Ads, text or banners adverts. If the ads are from your competitors, save, record and document them.

To document these and keep track of them, I recommend you track these ads. Create a "print screen" of these ads by pressing the PrtSc button on Windows or pressing Shift-Command (⌘)-3 on a Mac, and paste them into a Word document, *known as a swipe file*, to reference them at a later time.

Check out the Top 10 on Google for a given keyword phrase. Also, look at Facebook ads that stand out, niche websites or forums with banner ads. Collecting and collating this information as a part of your research will be invaluable when it comes to competitor analysis.

Research – Front End

After capturing the "print screens" of your competitor's ad, click on the ad and then visit the pages associated with it. Look at the design and take note of what you like and dislike on the page. Read the copy (text) in the headline, sub headline, and main content and consider how it reads and if it works well.

What are they offering and what is the Call To Action? Is it lead generation (name and email opt-in)? Ecommerce or add to cart with secure payment online? Solely information, brand or audience building content?

It's important to take note of this information because for the most part, how your competitors advertise on the front end with landing pages or other content is only 5-10% of what their business offers.

This is usually referred to as the Front-End. Don't be fooled in thinking that this is all they do. Most successful coaching businesses have front end offers that gather leads, prospects and customers.

However, their main goal is what they can offer and upsell once they've collected the data of the prospect, on-boarded or after having successfully closed the client.

Research – Back End

The Back-End is where the profit and lifetime value of your customer can be realised. It's where your product range can be fully offered, and then sold, bringing in more revenue and profit.

Surveys – Getting insight directly from your target market, a survey can unlock what your leads are thinking before they become a prospect and then eventually a client. I've sent leads straight to a survey to qualify them as prospects. I've asked prospects to fill out surveys and qualify them before meetings. As part of online marketing campaigns, I've covertly used them to get people to move to another stage in my marketing funnel.

Every time I use surveys, they work. An important point to note... You don't need hundreds or thousands of people to fill them out in order for them to be useful or to get answers to your customers' biggest needs or problems.

The goal of the survey is to get the answers you need to plan the next step in your marketing and sales. They also get your prospects to think about their business in a more open and visionary manner.

Sometimes the questions in the survey are usually the ones that prospects avoid or don't want to answer. The questions make them pause, and they start to think and look at what they really want. You unleash the entrepreneur in them, "give them space to think", which in turn accelerates what you need.

Offline

Joint Venture (JV's) – These are generally companies who have lists of people that can be targeted through email, remarketed online advertisements or offline tactics. A joint venture works based on you partnering with someone that has a list of your preferred (target) audience. In exchange for access to the list, the joint venture partner will charge you a fee or require a percentage of your sales for everyone who buys your product/service.

Strategic Partners – Companies who serve your audience with different non-competing products or services. They may allow you to use or target their list in exchange for you returning the favour. These can be very powerful for longer term relationships.

Books – One of the oldest and most powerful ways to perform your research is to get insight from the books your target market is buying. Read and reviewing up to ten of the best sellers will give you deep insight.

Newspapers & Magazines – These mediums give you a glimpse into the recent activity in a marketplace. Buy a few copies each month for several months to spot the trends in the market. Take note of the advertisers who show up regularly and their message. For maximum impact, contact the advertising executives of the magazines and newspapers that tailor to your audience. They may reveal more insight into how well those advertisers are doing in terms of sales performance and brand building.

Competitor Ads – Create a scrap book of your competitor's ads. Don't see them as competitors, but collaborators. It doesn't matter if they are direct competitors or serve your potential customers in different ways from you. The more you get insight of what's going on in your industry, the better and more prepared you are to offer your services.

Radio – Listen to the ads that appear during radio programs or at specific intervals in a show (whether via traditional FM radio or via an online streaming service offered by the station). Track the trends of the companies who advertise and take not of their ad style, the scripting and Call-to-Action.

Competitor Research Critical Analysis

As you're looking at your competitors, their messaging (copy) and call to action, there are other points to consider to get very detailed insight. Here is a list of specific points to analyse and document in your research file about your competitors:

- **Hook** – What is their hook or headline? What idea or angle are they using to attract clients and get the market's attention?
- **Primary Marketing Promise** – What is the primary promise of their marketing? (Speed, results, etc.)
- **Vehicle** – What is the key way they deliver their product or service? Is there a unique mechanism, process, component, piece or method they use? Is it existing or unique?
- **Unique Selling Proposition** – What is the main benefit they offer for using the product or service?
- **Marketing Claims** – What are their claims?
- **Proof Points** – How are they proving their claims? Social proof via testimonials, case studies, research data etc? What makes the proof credible?
- **Benefit Statements** – What benefits do they display on their sales pages, website and promotions? How does this help your target audience in their life or business?
- **Deliverables/Features** – What do they offer as a distinctive attribute or aspect of the product or service?
- **Price & Terms** – What is their pricing? Is it high or low? How is it offered - one payment, monthly payments, staged payments, interest free, buy now/pay later? Do their prices make sense from a profitability perspective? Are their prices used as loss leaders *(A product or service that is offered at a price that is not profitable, but is sold or offered in order to attract new customers or to sell additional products and services to those customers. In the hope of securing future revenues)* or trip wires to start the client buying process?
- **Bonuses/Premiums** – Do they include bonuses or premiums (digital or physical)? Do the bonuses address additional problems

that the client will come across that the core product doesn't cover?

- **Guarantees** – How do they reverse the risk of their offering and make their offer more appealing to prospects? What are the terms of their guarantee? How does it work - cash back, satisfaction, or evidence-based (client has to do something first)? What they're offering and not offering?

To get the best results for your business, you must pay attention to this information. Take notes and save this information in your research document, log or journal. Why? Because you're looking for the gaps and the angle that you can use to penetrate the market with your own niche. You're looking at where the competition is in the market compared to you so that you can create a plan to dominate rather than compete.

Assembling A Swipe File

Using all the data you've gathered, you'll need to create a file that contains everything to do with ads, videos, pictures and content. This is referred to as a Swipe File. This is what should be included:

1. Target audience locations (included, Google keyword data, Facebook insights and any lists you acquired from different sources)
2. Copies of direct marketing ads that other people have used in your market related to what you intend to offer or sell.
3. Copies of books, magazines, and reports on the sub market *(we'll come to this shortly)* you are aiming at.
4. Copies of really good ads and marketing pieces, even if they are not related to your specific product or service.
5. Anything else that will help you to generate ideas.

Review the information in your swipe file and find the common themes. Use similar language and align your product or service to what's trending. Write down the explanations and ideas you get from this information. This priceless insight will help you form the creative ideas that will be used in your marketing campaigns. It will aid you in getting clarity on your customer's desires and allow you to drive home a message of the value you add to them. You'll be able to demonstrate a true understanding of what the market is doing and understand the messages you should be working on based on existing messages that are generating results.

Additional Questions to ask yourself about your product or service

Now that you've gathered the information about your market, you need to dig deeper into your target audience's desires, fears, emotions and motivations. This will reveal how you position your products and services to persuade them to take action.

- What is their specific problem?
- What is their point of desperation?
- What is their dominant resident emotion? *(Fear, Anger, Joy, Trust, Love etc)*
- What is the main emotional state they have entering the marketing campaign?
    - Excitement, fear, scarcity
- What keeps them up at night?
- What is their internal dialogue saying?
- What are they not saying, but sub-consciously they are? *(What are they most ashamed about, and they don't really want to reveal to anyone)*

These questions allow you to dig deeper, into truly knowing your target audience, your niche…Knowing what will trigger them to making a decision to find out more about you, your product and ultimately buy from you.

How to Define Your Market & Niche

When it comes to defining your market, there are 3 core markets that everyone generally fits into. They are:

1. Wealth
2. Health
3. Relationships

Once you've defined which market you belong to, you need to then choose a hot submarket. And when I say "hot," I mean there are already customers in this market buying similar products and services. This will be a sure-fire indicator that you're at least looking in the right direction.

Why is this important?

Instead of trying to come up with a completely different market, which is nearly impossible, the best thing to do is go where there's already action.

So let's use some examples of markets and submarkets;

1. Wealth
   - Online Business, Accountancy, Builder / Contractor, Lawyer, Coaching, Clothing & Apparel, Travel
2. Health
   - Fitness, Weight loss, Athletics, Diet, Cooking
3. Relationships
   - Dating, Marriage, Parenting, Counselling, Family

Starting with the 3 overarching markets and further defining a submarket will allow you to drill down a little more and create a "niche".

According to Britannica;

> *"A niche is defined as a small target group that has special requirements. For example, a bank may specialize in serving the investment needs of not only senior citizens, but also*

senior citizens with high incomes and perhaps even those with particular investment preferences."

Why create a niche? You not only want to go into a hot-market but you want stand out in the right way so that potential prospects can see how you're different. You want them to see your unique selling points, unique mechanisms and unique message.

You should take into consideration the key attributes of your target audience, then add to it "a small, specialized section of the population" (demographics and interests they have) and then psychographics ("why" they buy). This allows you to filter them down and clearly define a niche of your own.

Some examples of how you can "niche down" would include, choosing

- Gender (male/female)
- Age (30-55)
- Relationship Status (single, married, divorced, civil partnership)
- Location (continent, country, region, city, town)
- Languages
- Financial
- Home Ownership Status
- Interests (Books, Magazines, Clothing Brands, Groups, Memberships, Buying Habits), etc
- Where are they in their lives right now?
- What do they want?
- What makes them angry?
- What do they fear?
- What are their Passions?

You should start marketing as soon as possible. However, identifying your niche will save you years of pain and frustration from using the wrong marketing message and having to speak to wrongly qualified prospects – tire kickers. By defining your niche you'll avoid sleepless nights, money wasted and stress!

Pitching Yourself to People

While attending networking events with business owners, you can introduce yourself several ways. Either you use the information introduced earlier, or you can do it the generic way. For example: I can introduce myself, I get to meet a few people and then introduce myself...

"Hi, I'm Leon Streete. I have a marketing agency, and I help business owners with online marketing."

What did you learn about the services offered in this introduction? How many other online marketers and web designers are at this networking event and are pitching the same business owners?

In order to stand out and become more memorable in the minds of the target market, the pitch should also include several other factors, including the market and niche.

1) Market & sub-market:
   - Wealth → Personal Development
2) The niche:
   - Online marketing for established business and life coaches who want to create 6-7 figure marketing campaigns

Incorporating the marketing and the niche creates a different pitch. Consider the following:

"Hi, I'm Leon Streete. I help established business and life coaches who are looking to position their business as authorities in their niche and most importantly achieve this through using a proven marketing system. I help them create 6-7 figure marketing campaigns that result in consistent lead generation and high-value sales, which gives them leverage and reward in their life and business."

See the difference?

- There is clarity on who is helped– established business and life coaches
- How they are helped – lead gen & high-value sales

- Specific niche characteristics – established coached with a 6 -7 figure marketing goal
- In a specific market – personal development

When the marketing tactics are properly employed, there's a clear focus and MESSAGE.

Having clarity on your elevator pitch keeps the focus on the niche you serve. Many times, coaches lose focus and switch niches. They end up going back to using the general approach instead of a niche, and their undesired results reflect it.

Below are some examples of creating an elevator pitch.

Market: Wealth → Coaching → Niche: Female executives 40-50 leadership
Old: I'm a leadership Coach for women **New:** When you're an executive level woman in your 40's, you start to wonder if all the sacrifices you made to achieve success were worth it. You're exhausted and tired of playing office politics to get ahead and want to live a more meaningful and peaceful life. Personal relationships may have suffered over the years and you're wondering how can everything feel so twisted on the inside even though everyone sees you as a raving success on the outside. I assist women with shifting from success to significance by connecting to their deeper calling, which can lead to a career promotion, transitioning to another job or starting a small business – using the skills and resources you already possess. I do this through my "Equilibrio Program," the only coaching method in the world that allows ambitious executive women to finally live with total clarity, to purposefully pursue your vision, where your career turns an exciting corner, your relationships are thrilling and stronger, and you're creating a life you had only ever thought possible in your dreams.

Market: Wealth → Online Business → Niche: Business Owners 35-55 with a £2m+ online business
Old: I'm a Marketing Coach. I help Coaches (Business, Life, Executive, Leadership, and Relationship) **New:** Running your own coaching business can be very rewarding, but many face a much tougher experience. Coaches aged 30-60 often feel frustrated with the low amount of leads they attract each week. Networking isn't working, and their online ads lose money. The feel like they're banging their heads against a wall. I help you figure out marketing so you're increasing leads through my "Vortex V3 methodology," in the only exclusive "Elevation" programme. Specifically created to allow coaches at the £250k+ mark, to generate leads on demand. Also, make sales and finally live the lifestyle they desire without overwhelm or technology holding them back.

Market: Wealth → Corporate Business → Niche: High Net worth Executives in London
Old: I'm a Management Coach. **New:** Hi I'm Wendy, I help women aged 30-50 in HR and Management roles, in businesses with 10+ employees, where they gain self-belief, confidence and leadership when it comes to people management. Management with authenticity is not a natural skill – it can be frustrating, leave you underappreciated and lonely at best. But I show women how to get it right and grow a business through strength in team whilst being a leader and adding fun.

Market: Health → Corporate Foreign Leadership → Niche: Executives aged 35-45
Old: I'm an executive coach. **New:** I work with Western Business Leaders aged 35 - 45 who have taken on a role as Country Manager, General Manager, Regional Manager in complex markets in Far East Asia. They are feeling very much under pressure because the local market situation is very complex and difficult to navigate, and the Headquarters have high expectations on them. They are worried and not sure about what they need to do. They find themselves micromanaging and the more talented employees leave the company, turnover is high, they're afraid that the stakeholders may lose trust in their abilities. This makes them feel frustrated, stressed and keeps them awake at night. This has an impact on the relationship with their family, because they spend a lot of time at work, and even when they are at home they are thinking about the business. As an experienced Global Business and Leadership Coach I help them to accelerate business and organizational success in Far Eastern Markets by building trust with their different stake holders fast, and making effective strategic decisions. I do this exclusively through my "Global Dynamics" programme, designed and created to lead you to success using my unique "3x3 Global Leadership Methodology".

Market: Health → Pregnancy → Niche: Couples & Women, mid 30's having difficulty getting pregnant
Old: I'm an Ayurveda Doctor. **New:** Getting pregnant is an emotional and lonely journey. Women in their mid-30's often feel depressed, unfulfilled, scared, confused, heartbroken, overwhelmed and defeated. At Ashishveda Fertility, we hold the hands of women during these vulnerable times so they can walk their fertility journey calmly. We support women physically, mentally and emotionally while they go through our "Five Step Rasayana Process" in the only Exclusive Ananda programme created by me, Dr Ashish Paul, an Ayurveda Doctor.

Market: Wealth → Business Owners → Niche: creative entrepreneurs aged 30-40
Old: I'm an ADHD Coach. **New:** I work with successful creative business owners and executives aged 30-40 who are feeling overwhelmed, and feel they are floating through life. They feel unfulfilled, and stressed, they wish to strengthen their personal systems and regain their inner clarity, vision, and peace of mind, and to live their life towards their purpose. At Focus With Faigy we'll work together to help you make that a reality. I support you as you go through the 5 Step Discovery Process exclusively available in the "Vision Program", the only program in the world that opens the door to earn your dream income and lifestyle. Created by me Faigy Liebermann – "The Success Coach".

Product, Pricing, Packaging& Placement

As a marketing coach I regularly cover this topic with both new and existing coaches. And often the line they say to me is, "I'm not sure where to start with my product (or service). What should be included? How I should price it? and how should I package it?"

Product - When you get to the stage of creating your product you need to pay attention to the needs of your clients. With your research performed and still on-going as you gather feedback and monitor performance over time, you will know (1) what your product or service will deliver as its core promise, (2) the benefits it offers, (3) the features it has and (4) the results it will help your customers achieve in their life and business.

There are some simple steps you can take to get your product off the ground, and it's important that you follow each step to ensure it starts off on the right foundation. These steps are:

1. Product Description, 2. Pricing, 3. Packaging

Product Description

Write down a paragraph description of your product (service) including the main features, options, modules and sessions it covers. If it's an information product, you need to include the number of lessons, videos, and audio and any documents it contains.

Next, write down what the product will do for you. Will it make you wealthy? How will more money in your business help you to serve your customers at a higher level or provide more value? Will, your clients, be able to increase their status, have more money in their bank account, buy a car, buy a house, take more holidays or simply have more time to do things outside of business? If the answer is yes, write it down.

Pricing

The most common pricing I see from business owners, coaches and consultants is;

- By The Session (e.g. £100/session)
- By The Month (e.g. £1000/month)
- By The Package (e.g. 6 month package for £5000)

As a Coach, the most profitable way to get your business moving is to offer a high-value service or product. Generally something with a price of £2000 or more. If you're not charging this amount for any of your services or products, you need to consider some basic math.

Example 1: If you have a £3000 product or service and let's say it lasts 8 weeks and you're trying to achieve a goal of £10,000 a month – you will need 7 clients. The basic numbers would simply be:

- £3,000 x 7 clients = £21,000
- 8 weeks = 2 months
- £20,000 / 2 months = £10,000 a month

Example 2: If you have a £500 product or service and it lasts over an 8 week period, and you're trying to hit £10,000 a month – you will need 40 Clients. Here are the numbers;

- £500 x 40 clients = £20,000
- 8 weeks = 2 months
- £20,000/2 months = £10,000 a month

The difference with the lower priced product is that you will need to do more work to sell your service since you are targeting nearly six times the number of customers (40).

This simple explanation demonstrates that by knowing the numbers before you get into your programme can save you a lot of extra work and effort than lower priced products. Momentum is key when you're growing and scaling your business, and if you have less people that you're targeting with a higher price point, you can move forward in your business with more confidence as you convert more clients into your programme.

Hopefully, you understand the difference between low and high-value products and have chosen to create a high-value product to propel your marketing campaigns beyond the 6-figure stage. At the very least, you've started with the right price point. If you've chosen a lower priced product be clear that you can hit the total client numbers needed to reach your targets.

Quick story – Meet Dr Ashish Paul: I spoke to her as she was faced with the conundrum of pricing per hour against raising her prices based on the value and results she delivered. She's a doctor and hard working single mother of two and her income wasn't sufficient. She was still dependant on income from other sources in addition to what her business was generating. When I spoke with her, our conversion went like this…

"I'm not sure about raising my prices, or how people will respond."

Instead of worrying about pricing, I got her to look at how she described her service, the package she offered and finally, the price. By the time we made the adjustments, we raised her price from nearly £1000 to £2895 – a 300% increase! We named it the "Ānanda Programme" that contained a unique mechanism the "Rasāyana Process." Her signature programme was complete and unique in the marketplace. After only one month of marketing, she'd gone from an average of £2500 per month in sales to £8685 with only 3 new clients!

Packaging

Now that your product is outlined and your pricing is ready, this is a quick 4 step process you can use for packaging (whether you sell products, services or coaching).

Step 1: Start by defining what your product/service will be. Will it be aone off purchase product, on-going maintenance, one-to-one coaching, group coaching or a self-study course etc. With these factors in mind, determine how much time the individual client will receive (number of visits, number of months, number of sessions/month and length of sessions).

The decision on how much time you'll offer for customer care/ coaching should be based on how you will best support your clients in achieving the result they desire. This may be tough if you're a start-up, so writing this down will get you to think and come up with what's right for now.

For physical products, detailing the estimated delivery time and demo products will go a long way to help convince your prospects. For coaches, most 1-to-1 and group coaching programmes should range from 6, 8 or 10 weeks or 3-12 months. Consider how much coaching you will provide time permitting and how much coaching (the length of time) clients will sign up for.

Step 2: What will you include with your product/programme? What main features will you include with your product, service or programme? What are the benefits of each feature?

From your research and any surveys you create, I recommend:

- Answering the questions of your prospects biggest challenges.
- The answers can be grouped together to form a common theme of questions. Then, they can be turned into your key points of products/service delivery or coaching modules.
- Next, make a welcome package or introduction video. You want clients to become accustomed to the rules of your business. What I like to call, "rules of the game." This should set the scene of where you're taking them and what will be included in each session
- Finally, tell them the first action they need to take to get them moving toward their desired result.

Step 3: Determine what additional services, value-added premiums or bonuses you want to include. For example: upsells, follow-up home visits, extra care products, 1-to-1 strategy calls, guides, workbooks, assessments, recorded video explainers or coaching sessions, written reports, other services such as consulting, "done-for-you" or "done-with-you" services, etc.

Step 4: Price your products and programmes. Collate your research so your market, niche, competition and related sources are pooled together, and you can see what the market is currently offering. I recommend you price yourself in the medium to high bracket. Never start cheap (bottom). It will cause you more headaches and put you in a place of price comparison, rather than prospects judging you on the value they will receive from you.

The final step is to create a guarantee (reverse your prospects risk), can you offer a money back guarantee or service-based guarantee. Consider linking a guarantee to specific actions the client must do in order to prove validity of any claim (this works well for coaches and consultants).

Placement

Choosing the right place is crucial for selling your products or services. There are many places and channels to sell what you have, and I recommend you focus on where there are already buyers of similar services/competitors in the market. Don't overcomplicate where to find your target audience.

Look at both offline and online activities. Offline may include networking events, speaking opportunities, Joint Venture partners, direct mail, expos or trade shows, etc. Online will include using places like Facebook, LinkedIn, Google, Forums and Email Marketing.

Now that you've gone through the 4P's analysis, it's time to put it against the market to understand the level of awareness and sophistication your message needs to have.

Market Awareness and Sophistication

Most markets don't share the same awareness nor are they equal. "Awareness Level and the Market Sophistication" will allow you to fully understand your audience. These two phrases come from the late great Gene Schwartz and his book "Breakthrough Advertising" published in 1966.

Market Awareness Scale

Every market has different levels of awareness. The more aware you are of your market, the easier it will be to market and sell…and the less you need to say (e.g. in your headlines)

1. The Most Aware – The customer knows of your product.
2. Product Aware – The customer knows of your product but doesn't yet want it.
3. New Products – The prospect either knows or recognises immediately that they want what the product does, but they don't know there is a product – I.e. your product
4. Problem Aware – The prospect has a need. They know it immediately, but don't know that your product fulfils the need.
5. Completely Unaware – The prospect is either not aware of their desire or need, or they won't honestly admit it to themselves without being lead into it by your ad.

The 5 Levels of Market Sophistication;

The five levels of sophistication allow you to identify how refined your target audience is based on the research you've already carried out. You can look at the types of ads your competitors are running and where people are buying. Based on this identification, you can plan the level of messaging you will need to use in your marketing campaigns.

Level 1 – The claim (take this spill and lose weight)

Level 2 – Expansion of the claim (lose 10lbs in 4 weeks)

Level 3 – Introduce a Unique Mechanism (Vortex V3 methodology)

Examples of Unique mechanisms;

1. Gillette – Fusion ProGlide Razor with "FlexBall Technology".
2. Olay – Anti-Wrinkle 2in1 Moisturiser uses "special light-reflective particles".
3. Book – Zero Limits: The "Secret Hawaiian System" for Wealth, Health, Peace, and More.

Level 4 – Expand on the Mechanism (The Coaches Solution for 6-7 figure Campaigns)

Level 5 – It's Now about the prospect

E.g. Are you…

It's more about the competitors/products already in the market

With knowledge of awareness and sophistication, you have an insider's view of your target audience. This understanding is priceless in the planning and marketing stage of what you're about to create with your advertising campaigns, headlines, content and products.

Persuasion… The job of your ads is to persuade prospects into buying what you're advertising, and this level of understanding is key, as you will soon notice the majority of what your competition and market are doing will be of a lesser level of awareness compared to you. You will find ads and competitors talking about themselves totally missing that fact that the target customer is only interested in themselves. And from what you just learned you are already one step ahead of the competition.

Persuasion comes in two parts;

- Emotion
- Logic

The caveat – when I talk of persuasion, it's from a place of integrity. For example, if someone was stuck in a burning building on the second floor and I wanted to help them escape, "I would persuade them" to jump into the safety blanket. With this in mind, your job is to seduce the heart (emotion)and convince the brain (intellect) in an ethical manner.

Now it's time to move onto building emotion through what makes you unique in the market.

How To Create a USP (Unique Selling Proposition)

The Unique Selling Proposition (USP) is also known as a Unique Value Proposition (UVP). The key question you must answer is... Why should I (your prospect) do business with you versus all other options, including doing nothing at all?

Roser Reeves, author of "Reality in Advertising", coined the term USP to describe the major advantage of your product over the competition.

According to Roser, there were three requirements of a USP.

1. Each advertisement must make a proposition to the consumer. Each must say, "Buy this product, and you will get this specific benefit." Your headline must contain a benefit – a promise to hook the reader
2. The proposition must be one that the competition either cannot or does not, offer.
3. The proposition must be so strong that it can move the mass millions, i.e.attract new customers to your product.

A USP is also a way of summarizing and portraying one of the top level benefits, often the chief benefit of the business, product, or service being marketed.

Your USP may express the "theme" or "culture" of your business, product, or service.

It can be based on price, product ingredient, or positioning. There are USPs based on colour, size, scent, celebrity endorsements, location, hours of operation, and so on.

Examples of USPs

1. FedEx Corporation – When it absolutely, positively has to be there overnight.
2. M&Ms – The milk chocolate melts in your mouth, not in your hand.
3. DeBeers – A diamond is forever.
4. Domino's Pizza – You get fresh, hot pizza delivered to your door in 30 minutes or less or it's free.
5. TOMS Shoes – are quirky, comfy, light and inexpensive. That alone maybe isn't enough to make a company stand out in the shoe business. The most unique and compelling part of the TOMS Shoes story is that they give a new pair of shoes to a child in need for every pair you purchase.

How to create your USP

This will not be a quick exercise, so don't expect to get it done within 10 minutes. The more you explore ideas, see different things in or outside of your market, it will come to you. You have to be persistent and work through them. Until you finalise the USP, use the best benefit you have until it is nailed down. Here are some tips to get you started.

- Put yourself in your customer's shoes.
- Know what motivates your customers' behaviour and buying decisions.
- Uncover the real reasons customers buy your product instead of a competitor's. Your research should help to reveal this.
- Use the features/benefits table ***listed in chapter 3*** – "Sales Letters," to help you uncover the main benefit that will fulfill your prospect's desires. You can include it in your USP below.

USP Formula:

USP = The ***Enabler*** + The Main ***Benefit***

Elevation is the only Programme designed to allow Coaches at the £250k+ mark, to generate leads on demand, make sales and live the lifestyle you desire without overwhelm, a poor strategy or technology holding you back...

With your USP created it's now time to put together your marketing plan.

What is a Marketing Plan?

Your marketing plan is *HOW* you are going to achieve those marketing goals. It's the application of your strategy and a plan that will guide you from one point to your destination.

Your marketing plan should include:

- **Message Topics** – The topics you want to cover.
- **Content Styles** – The type of content you plan to produce (i.e. blog posts, videos, infographics, etc).
- **Schedule (Time Plan)** – A timeline that details what content will be published.
- **Responsibilities** – Who is responsible for your content (creation, editing, and publishing).
- **The Marketing Mix** – All of the activities (tactics) that gets your message in front of your target-audience: paid ads, social media, webinars, seminars, podcast, email marketing, etc.

Remember... Be fluid like water, be flexible, and ready to adapt. There are many situations that can occur and impact your plan. This is life. Things change and it's your job to keep your eye on the prize and enjoy the journey. It may sound cliché, but that's how it is.

The following sections of the Marketing Plan are listed to guide you in what you will need to cover. However, there is one important ***MUST-DO*** principle – **You must write this down or type it up, there must be some evidence of it existing beyond yours or your team's mind. If it isn't written down, it will remain an idea, not an actionable plan.**

How to Create Your Marketing Plan, Step By Step

1. With your strategy created, you can now transform it into a marketing plan.
2. The plan goes into the logistical details of executing your strategy, such as budgets, more detailed timescales, who within your company will manage the various points of the strategy, the management of various marketing channels and the incurred costs, customer acquisition cost and so on.
3. The plan is a longer and more detailed document than the strategy.
4. Your marketing plan is typically a more active document than your strategy (meaning you will tweak and update it more regularly). As costs, market conditions, economic conditions and other factors change, you'll need to adjust your plan to accommodate them - whereas your strategy may well remain the same.
5. For both your strategy and your plan to be useful, you need to closely monitor the results of marketing activity.

Why Finding A Niche With Problems &Needs Is Critical

The fastest way to sell and make money is to fix a person's problem by offering them a solution or serve their needs. It sounds simple, but it's the simplicity of this statement that most people take for granted.

People think they need a bunch of stuff in place first before they can start marketing and selling. Such as a logo, website, marketing funnel, email automation, sales presentation, testimonials, sales script, paid advertising, a great or "perfect" product etc.

The reality is that all of this adds power and weight in your ability to increase leads, conversions, and profitability – but it's not necessary to get started.

** Let me share a story

As a 23-year-old, I had a hobby business where I created websites and back then we didn't have fancy WordPress Websites or Marketing Funnel tools. We created websites from HTML and Programming pages.

I was hungry to show the world what I could do and I knew I could help people fix their problem of having a website, so I did what any respectable "A-Team" viewer would do. I devised a strategy and made a plan (a very small one at that) and targeted shops I knew I could help. I checked to see if they had websites and whether or not they did, I would go and ask to speak to the owner. No appointments. I just turned up!

I walked to the businesses (I wasn't driving back then) and said, "Hi I'm Leon Streete, I run a web design company and help business owners get online without any tech headache and in an easy way that helps to market your business."

Pretty simple and at the time it was all I needed. I ended up with some people saying they were not interested, whilst others wanted to talk more and learn more about what was possible for them. (If I had known about how to qualify at this point, it would have saved me a lot of time. Oh well… I learnt how to communicate better with prospects!) Eventually, I came across people who were really into the idea and wanted to know the next steps.

I secured my first client off the back of cold canvassing. An ecommerce client by the name of Huckleberry's Menswear. The owner was Steve, really great guy who taught me a lot about client relationships, seasonal buying, trends in retail as well as how to present your business. He became a 10 year client, and more clients followed.

These were the signals I was looking for, and it helped me realize I could *sell* a solution. It was exciting, fun, and new and I was filled with confidence.

CHAPTER ACTION SUMMARY

What you need to put into Action

- **Marketing Strategy**
  - The Goal – What's the target?
  - Market – Choose the market.
  - Niche – Carve out a niche to dominate.
  - Research – Understand what's in the market and how its moving.
  - Elevator Pitch – What to say.
  - 4P's – What your product must include.
  - Market Sophistication – what level do you need to be at?
  - USP – Your main product benefit.
- **Marketing Plan**
  - Create the logistics, details and tactics that must be actioned

Refer to the MLMC Workbook to work on these key points.
www.moreleadsmoreclientsbook.com/resources

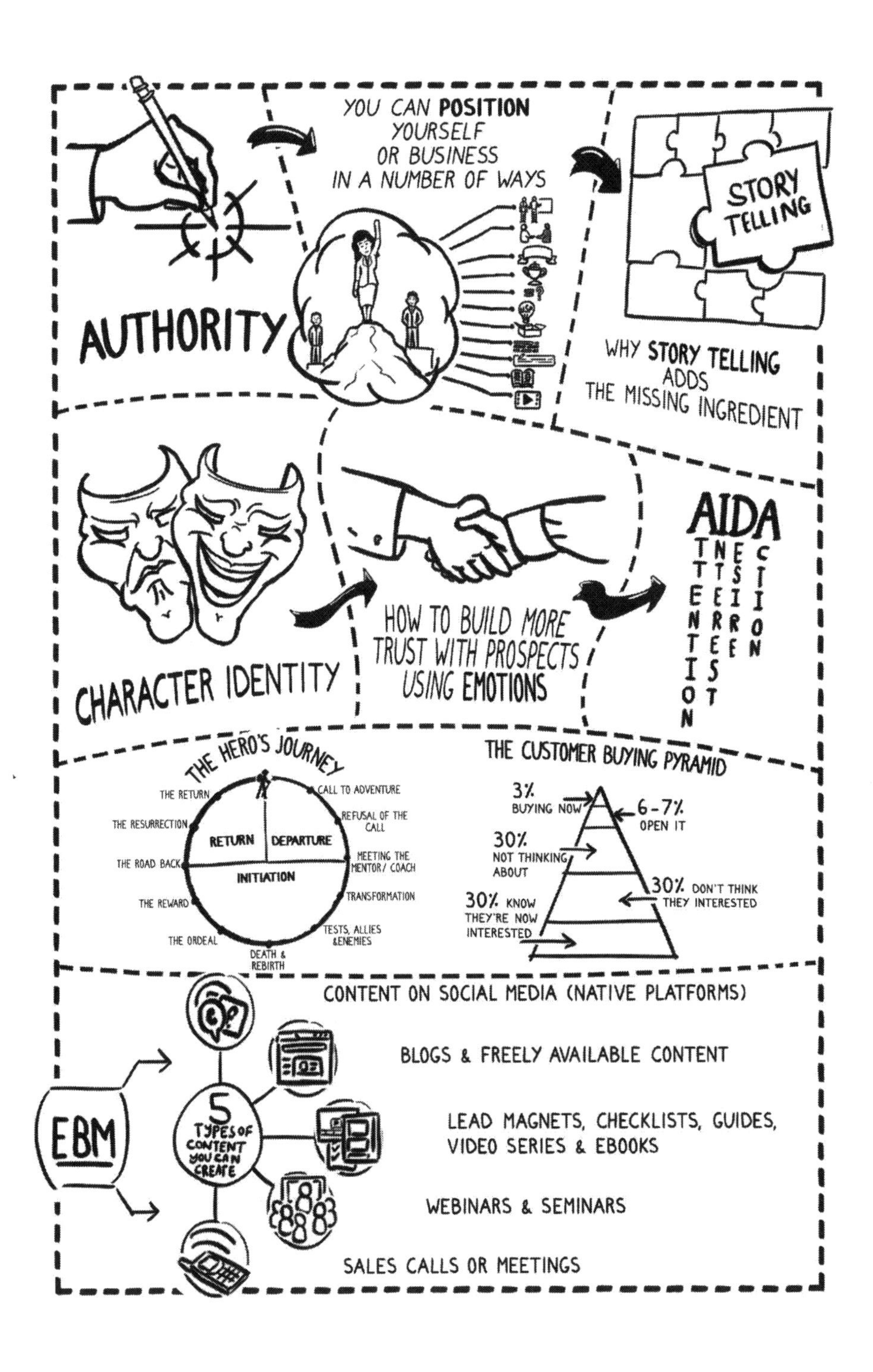

AUTHORITY
YOU CAN POSITION YOURSELF OR BUSINESS IN A NUMBER OF WAYS
STORY TELLING
WHY STORY TELLING ADDS THE MISSING INGREDIENT
CHARACTER IDENTITY
HOW TO BUILD MORE TRUST WITH PROSPECTS USING EMOTIONS
AIDA
ATTENTION
INTEREST
DESIRE
ACTION
THE HERO'S JOURNEY
CALL TO ADVENTURE
REFUSAL OF THE CALL
MEETING THE MENTOR/ COACH
TRANSFORMATION
TESTS, ALLIES &ENEMIES
DEATH & REBIRTH
THE ORDEAL
THE REWARD
THE ROAD BACK
THE RESURRECTION
THE RETURN
RETURN
DEPARTURE
INITIATION
THE CUSTOMER BUYING PYRAMID
3% BUYING NOW
6-7% OPEN IT
30% NOT THINKING ABOUT
30% DON'T THINK THEY INTERESTED
30% KNOW THEY'RE NOW INTERESTED
EBM
5 TYPES OF CONTENT YOU CAN CREATE
CONTENT ON SOCIAL MEDIA (NATIVE PLATFORMS)
BLOGS & FREELY AVAILABLE CONTENT
LEAD MAGNETS, CHECKLISTS, GUIDES, VIDEO SERIES & EBOOKS
WEBINARS & SEMINARS
SALES CALLS OR MEETINGS

CHAPTER 2

How To Position Yourself as an Authority

By now, you should have researched and thought about your strategy, target audience, and service or product. In the previous chapter, you learned how to create your social pitch and identified who you can specifically help. Taking these actions will get you past being stressed, frustrated, having unqualified leads, sleepless nights, and wasting your money!

You're probably asking, what else do I need to know?

Do you remember the social pitch?

> ***"Running your own coaching business can be very rewarding, but many face a much tougher experience. Coaches aged 30-60 often feel frustrated with the low amount of leads they attract each week. Networking isn't working, online ads are losing money, and it's like they're banging their heads against a wall.***
> ***I help you figure out marketing, so you're increasing leads through my "Vortex V3 methodology," in the only exclusive "Elevation" programme. Created to allow Coaches at the £250k+ mark, to generate leads on demand, make sales and finally live the lifestyle without overwhelm or technology holding them back."***

This is the first step. Identifying all the key components of what your target audience is looking for, but now let's pull the target audience in and get them to pay close attention to move them to the point where they are begging for more. To do that, you need to become the "Authority or Expert" in your niche.

There are many ways to create authority, the very word **AUTHOR**ity as you can see as I've highlighted contains the word "AUTHOR." Authority and expertise come as a result of creating something that your niche values. There are different ways to create value, both tangible and intangible, which is why positioning is also necessary.

Why use Positioning?

Positioning is a powerful piece of your marketing strategy. You want to make the right impression with the right people. If you do it right, people will want to listen to you and give you their time. When you properly deliver your content with personality, passion and culture, it will appeal to potential fans and prospects, and they will choose to become part of the community you create.

It's the difference between someone watching a video, reading a piece of content and even opting in for a lead magnet, as opposed to an actual paying client. The two are completely different and properly positioning you, your product and your culture will make this happen.

You can position yourself or business in a number of ways, here's a few to consider:

- **Association** – Who can you connect with? For example, when I interviewed guests on my podcasts I was able to use those guests, their brand presence and marketplace positing and put this out in my marketing to theirs and my advantage.
- **Joint Venture** – you partner with an organisation that endorses you and then markets your product or service to their customers or vice versa to increase reach and sales.

- **Title or naming** – Muhammad Ali said "I am the greatest" before he was the greatest – why was he the greatest, because of his achievements or because he indoctrinated everyone to this title he gave himself?
- **Awards** – Have you won an award that helps to add prestige to your brand? For some reason, people always hold awards that people have in higher regard.
- **Results** – Being the first to achieve a notable result, something that your customers want to also experience.
- **USP** – Use a powerful unique selling proposition to position yourself differently to your competition and in a highly competitive market
- **Products or Services** – that appear to be innovative have a unique piece, part or component, can stand out and allow you to be positioned differently from everyone else in the market.
- **Content**– that demonstrates why you care, demonstrating why you're the expert, demonstrating where your expertise came from, your experience related to the problem you help your niche solve, sharing your knowledge, sharing your experiences
- **Testimonials** – case studies, customer experiences
- **A Book** – Publishing a book (printed or digital (Kindle, etc)
- **Media** – Becoming a guest on a media outlet (podcast, radio, TV, etc),

Now that you have an angle, a position, you can now wrap it into a powerful story to truly build belief in your prospects around their desire to solve their number one challenge, with your service.

Why Story Telling Adds The Missing Ingredient

One of the main reasons stories are so good is that they are one of the most powerful forms of persuasion known to humans. Factstell, stories sell...

It's one of the most overlooked principles that many Coaches don't understand. The importance of introducing emotion to their prospect. For me, storytelling goes back to my childhood, where two of the best storytellers would fill my youthful imagination with stories of wonder, shock, awe and what was possible, These two great men were my granddad's. My father's dad was from Jamaica, and my mother's dad was from Wales.

And as a young mixed-race boy, this made for some interesting storytelling. Born in 1924, Alfred Streete was raised in a country known for its beauty, vibrant culture, tasty food, amazing warm and sunny weather, the infectious sounds of reggae music and of course, the rum! He was born to two hardworking parents in the countryside of a little place called Patty Hill in Hanover. His home was like a ram shackled wooden construction, with corrugated metal roofing and an abundance of resources, wood, food, fruit, and fish in the immediate surroundings.

He told me of his adventures, from catching fish and cooking them at the riverside with bread and fruit. Working his job and transporting wood to the local merchants on his trusty donkey (still boggles my mind now), to nights filled with drinking rum, playing high energy fuelled games of domino's and on occasion drunken fights (these stories I really enjoyed). Then there were stories of life lessons, understanding decision making, insights into some of the things I should look out for, be aware of, knowing when to see the angles, who to keep as company (who to hang around with). The journey of his voyage and transition from Jamaica to the UK in the late 1950's on the promise to rebuild post-war Britain and much more…

Born in 1926, William Batstone was raised in a country known for its idyllic countryside, its highest point mount Snowdon, the huge number of sheep and a place believed to have more castle per square mile than anywhere else in the world. He didn't talk much of his past in Wales. However, he would speak about his time in the British Royal Navy during World War II on a Mine Sweeper ship. As a young boy, I was engrossed – Hook, Line, and Sinker. To add further suspense and thrill to these stories, his ship hit a floating mine and left him and his fellow crew at sea for some time before they were rescued.

Granddad Batstone was a very consistent and methodical man. Very warm-hearted and looked out for people. He always welcomed whoever he came across with a smile on his face and instilled these types of principles in me as a young boy. I spent some fun times with my granddad on holidays, and his advice would be centred around, working hard, focusing on schoolwork and looking out for people, in particular, my mom. He was very chivalrous like that, and I was thankful I learned these things from both of my granddads.

It taught me from a young age, how powerful storytelling is for the mind. I could picture myself on warm beaches or by the river catching fish in Jamaica. What it was like to be marginalised based on racism and being on a Navy ship at sea fighting for your country. I remember hoping, even as a young boy, that one day I could tell such tales of wonder to my children and those who wanted to listen. And now my time has come.

Story Writing Methodology

When it comes to the method of writing and how to structure your content, there are at least 7 known methods to pen the perfect story that will engage your audience. They will get stories that thrill, excites, twists pulls at their emotions, takes them through crisis and back to the point of breakthrough, transformation, have new hope and conclusion.

Character Identity

The hero of your content will need a character identity. A character that your target audience can relate to. Remember, you are this character or at the very least, the spokesperson for your business.

Heroes

In the book, *The Hero with a Thousand Faces*, Joseph Campbell summarised the monomyth: A hero ventured forth from the world of common day into a region of supernatural wonder. Fabulous forces are encountered, and a decisive victory is won. The hero comes back from this mysterious adventure with the power to bestow boons on his fellow man.

In breaking down the monomyth, Campbell describes a number of stages along the hero's journey. The hero starts in the ordinary world and receives a calling to enter a new world of strange wonder and events (an adventure). If the hero accepts the call to enter this world, the hero must face tasks and trials. He/she may have to face these trials alone, or they may have assistance.

At its most intense stage, the hero must survive fabulous forces or severe challenge, often with help gained along the journey. If the hero survives, he/she may achieve a decisive victory (the goal or "boon"/ achievement), which often results in the discovery of important self-knowledge (transformation). The hero must then decide whether to return with this achievement (the return to the ordinary world), often facing challenges on the return journey. If the hero is successful in returning, the power of the achievement or gift may be used to bestow on their people (the application of the boon).

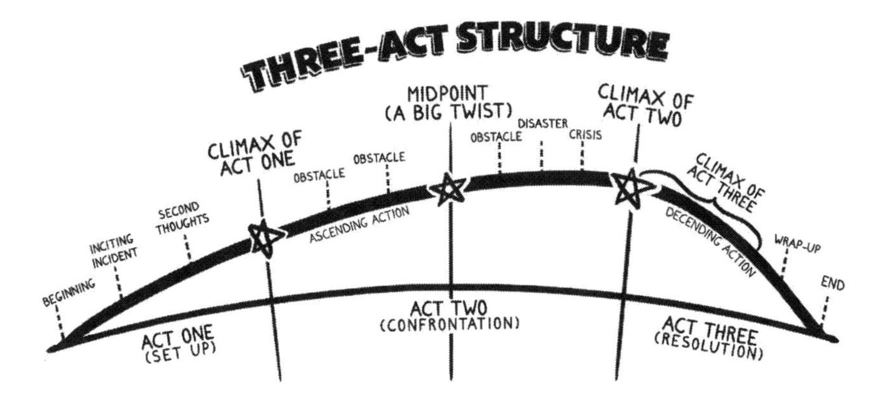

Famous movies such as Star Wars, The Lion King and The Matrix have all credited the influence of this monomyth (stages of the hero story). With this understanding, you can use three main stages to create your own story for your business, your products, and services. The stages are:

1. ***Departure.*** Take your audience on a journey of adventure. Tell them why you chose to create the business, product or service; how you tried to refuse the calling, but the market wouldn't go away; and how eventually your intuition or outside forces aided your decision to press forward and make a change.
2. ***Initiation.*** After taking on the calling, there are trials and tests, breaking through red tape, thinking outside of the box, rules, regulations, roadblocks, setbacks, pain, and sacrifice. Everything challenge that is sent allows you to either rise and conquer or find another path... However, with victory comes the reward – Achievement and Transformation.
3. ***Return.*** With victory achieved, it's time to return to your people (your audience). You are ready to share the gifts (knowledge, your products, and services). You can now re-position yourself as the master of two worlds. Through your victory, you now understand what it takes both internally and externally to achieve, and this has lead you to mastery and being able to live in the moment.

12 Archetypes

According to Carl Gustav Jung, there are 12 archetypes (characters) and each are made up of different elements and identities. Some of the most famed heroes fit into one of these archetypes: The Innocent, Regular Guy or Gal, The Hero, The Caregiver, The Explorer, The Rebel, The Lover, The Creator, The Jester, The Sage (mentor), The Magician(visionary) and The Ruler.

Which one are you? Not sure?

If you're stuck, that's okay. This is something that Russell Brunson breaks down in a much simpler format is his book, *Dot Com Secrets.* He uses the term Attractive Character (AC), and it is essentially the persona you will use to be more attractive in the eyes of your target audience.

The four identities he uses are (1) The Leader (2) The Adventurer (3) The Reporter/Evangelist and (4) The Reluctant Hero. What will attract your target audience to your character where they get to know you and will be ready to buy?

Here are a few businesses that use the AC concept. UK Bank, Halifax's hero, was Howard Brown. He was an actual customer service worker from the bank who sang and danced his way into the minds of the UK population on TV Adverts.

J'Adore Dior, fronted by CharlizeTheroncreated adverts across the world oozing with sophistication and sex appeal. Steve Jobs was the face of Apple for many years. His presence became synonymous with the idea of cool, innovative designed technology. With this in mind, you're now in a position where you can choose the types of storyline angle you can use in your content.

Storyline Angles

In business, using a storyline is a great way to open up the doors and appeal to your audience. Taking this route will give your conversation starting points and content openers that talk directly with your audience. They work time and time again like Hollywood blockbuster movies. Your goal is to use the examples given to give yourself the best possible start when it comes to communicating your message.

Story line examples

- **Us versus Them (David vs Goliath)** – Creating a polarised story that will allow people to buy into your culture, story or community. For example, Erin Brockovich, 51, is more than a mythic name to the residents of Hinkley, Calif., a small speck of a town on the edge of the Mojave Desert. She is the real-life hero who led the charge against their neighbourhood against a giant utility company, Pacific Gas and Electric, which contaminated the town's water supply in the 1950s and 60s
- **The Discovery** – Something new or re-discovered that people need to hear about. An example health article, scientists have heralded the "really exciting" discovery of a new process which triggers the death of cancer cells.
- **The Phoenix (From Failure to Rebirth)** – Steve Jobs found success in his 20s when Apple became a massive empire, but when he was 30, Apple's board of directors fired him. Undaunted by the failure, he founded a new company, NeXT, which was eventually acquired by Apple. Once back at Apple, Jobs proved his capacity for greatness by reinventing the company's image and taking the Apple brand to new heights.
- **Before and After– Old versus New**. Depicting transformation. Ursula Burns was raised by her single mother in a housing project. Her mother ran a day-care centre out of her home and ironed shirts so that she could afford to send Ursula to Catholic school. Ursula later went to NYU and became an intern at Xerox. She worked her way up the ladder and became Xerox's CEO and chairwoman. Burns was the first African-American woman to lead a Fortune 500 company.
- **The Secret** –The lure of the unknown. Something that shouldn't be revealed but is about to be. For example, there are seven essential principles that you must practice as an entrepreneur

throughout your business life if you want to achieve maximum success. They have been taught and repeated in only a few books and articles over the years, and here they are...

- **Character**– The movie series Indian Jones are not character stories. The story is always about what Indiana Jones does, but never who he is. Jones faces many problems and adventures, but in the end, his role in society is exactly what it was before, part-time archaeology professor and full-time knight-errant.
- **Disruption**– An effective way to hold a reader's attention is to disrupt their expectations, surprise them or swerve them away from what is generally considered to be the 'norm.' For example, behind every Google Map, there is a much more complex map that's the key to your queries but hidden from your view.
- **Quote Or Statistic** – If you're struggling for story angle, try using a quote or an interesting statistic. Using information from an external source can often help you catch the eye and hold a reader's attention. Check out this opening line from Fast Company, "Nearly 66% of companies on the Fortune 100 list in 1990 are not on the list some twenty-odd years later."
- **Story** – Use a story and add some intrigue and disruption. When a hitman pulled up beside Florian Homm's limousine and shot him in the chest, he did what any self-respecting hedge fund tycoon would have done, stuffed his wound with $100 bills and called his wife with a dying message – sell.

How To Build More Trust With Prospects Using Emotions

Now that your stories and content have an angle remember your goal for marketing is to build trust so that you can take a prospect from cold to sold. People buy after they've made an emotional decision to invest in something. To use this understanding to your advantage, you must inject the emotion by adding feelings into your content

To add feeling to your writing is a key component to engage your reader. You can also entertain your viewer through a video script or any content to speak directly to your audience. The process is simple yet often overlooked in the haste to "get campaigns and content out."

Use the idea of VAKOG - Visual, Auditory, Kinaesthetic (feel/touch), Olfactory (smell), Gustatory (taste). Write to engage your audience at the level of their feelings. This allows them to SEE when there isn't any visual presented; HEAR when there is no sound; FEEL when there is nothing but words, spoken or written; SMELL when there is no scent and finally TASTE when there is no food to sample.

An example to demonstrate.

> Tony sat in his office, yet his world was spinning out of control. The office phone was ringing, and voicemail was full from prior missed calls. He didn't hear anything and was zoned out from the noise whilst staring out the window as the world carried on. He was out of luck, out of ideas and finally out of money. The feeling of desperation had his stomach in knots. How could he tell his team they may lose their jobs and how could he explain to his wife that the business was going down and about to have a big impact on their young family financially. The guilt, disappointment, and the shame... He couldn't move. His chest became tight, and he couldn't breathe. His mouth was dry, and the smell of his uneaten lunch strangely made him feel like he wanted to throw up... What could he do? He had to find a way out of this situation...

In this example, I've added feeling and included the 5 human senses. There may be different parts in the example that you could relate to and could see in your mind. This is what you will need to add to your own messages and content.

I've even sat with clients who beforehand, explained "I can't make such claims or add in sensationalised bullshit," but afterwards they see it's nothing more than simply going beyond formal or boring writing. It's adding the emotion. With this in mind, you can now go after your target audience and capture their attention.

AIDA Formula

The AIDA formula = Attention, Interest, Desire, Action.
Attention – You put out a video on Social Media aimed at your target audience. When they see the video, *you get their attention*. This may be through a disruptive scene, picture or pattern interrupt that grabs attention.
Interest – With a properly formed message that speaks to the person's problem or need, they watch the video, demonstrating *you have their interest*, as the content becomes valuable to them.
Desire – As part of that video, your message includes a solution (product or programme) to their problem or need and it was delivered in a way that they could see the benefits of working with you as a coach. Now *they desire to have the solution* you are offering or selling.
Action – The final part is your Call-To-Action (CTA). You must offer a way that they can take the action required to have the solution. Your video must invite them to fill out an opt-in form by clicking on a button that leads them to a specific web page. When they have opted in, purchased online or something similar, you have achieved the *action required to get the result* you wanted.

The AIDA formula gets you to the next level of serving your clients' needs or solving a problem, e.g., upselling to the next programme or product. This type of ascension through your service or product offering is what we will cover next using the EBM formula.

EBM Formula

There two types of marketing - Feature/Offer Selling and Education Based Marketing (EBM). EBM is important to reaching your audience in the midst of their busy social media filled daily lives. A top sales trainer, Chet Holmes, discovered the buying habits of people at any given moment.

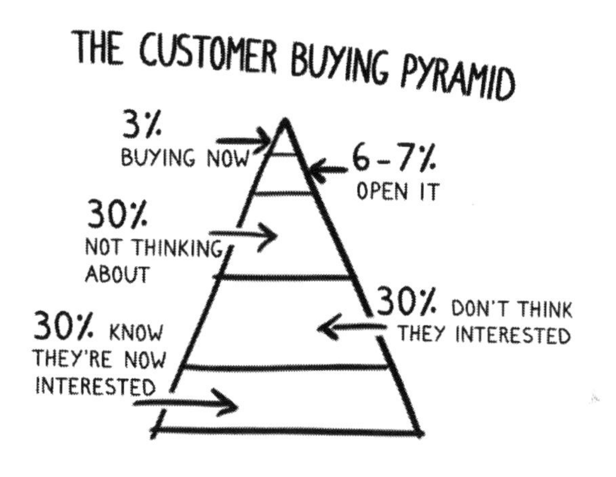

1. 3% are interested in buying "right now"
2. 7% are "open to consider such a purchase"
3. 30% are NOT thinking about it at this time
4. 30% don't "believe" they are interested (based on the info they have at hand)
5. 30% are definitely NOT interested

Something to consider is that there are people ready to buy now while others need warming up. With this in mind, you have to create a plan of content (education material) that you will use for people ready to buy now and those open to your offer. Also, for the majority, those who are not currently thinking about it and need warming up.

All too often, coaches only think about the first three levels, when their plan should be about all of them. If you can tap into 70% (the first 4 levels of the customer buying pyramid) and gain more customers from that group, you will create a bigger opportunity of increasing your marketing success.

Think about this for a moment. When it comes to prospects buying, you have to build their desire and establish belief. In order to do this you have to make a *claim*, back it up with *proof* and then *belief* is established. However, to bring your prospect to the point where they believe in buying your product or service, you have to trigger and establish all prerequisite beliefs to lead them to the main one.
It's like a draw by numbers picture. As you connect 1 to 2 and 2 to 3, the picture (the beliefs) are forming. Until you get to the final number and the picture is complete (the main belief established). Think of EBM content as the sequential numbers leading your prospects to buy.

Let's review more education based marketing to see what type of content can be created and why.

EBM Stage 1 – (Low risk / Safe Environment). When a lead (interested person) first comes across your content, you need to be aware of the place it occurs. E.g., If they see a post of your content on a social media website, they are on a place of their choosing, which is a place of low risk. They trust the environment and your message is an example of the first steps in increasing trust with you.

EBM Stage 2 – (Increased risk / Unknown Environment). If your social media content is accompanied by a link to your blog or some other web page and they choose to click that link, they choose to move away from the security of the platform to find out more. This holds true of a person searching on Google. They are seeking information and are willing to click on the search results not knowing if your company or the page they are about to visit is genuine. However, the answer to fix their problem or serve their need is worth the click (risk).

EBM Stage 3 – (Medium risk / Low Trust Environment). Once a lead has visited your opt-in page where you're offering a valuable piece of content (like an Ebook, guide or short video) in exchange for their name and email. Now the risk is medium. They've chosen to click to get to your page, but now they have to decide if the promise of the headline or the copy on the page is strong enough for them to give up their name and email. If they do, this is where you have established low trust, and they have risked more to get what you're offering.

EBM Stage 4 – (High risk / Trusted Environment). When your prospect (notice they have now transitioned from lead to prospect) has moved to a place where they have given their name, email and often a phone number, in exchange for valuable material, the next stage comes down to how much value the prospect places on what they have read or seen. If they have deemed your guide, Ebook or video to be of value, they should be willing to go to the next stage where they are willing to invest a pre-determined amount of time and schedule something into their diary. At this point, they will be willing to register for a Webinar (online seminar) or even attend a seminar in person (investing in, travel, time and possibly a low investment). At this stage, the risk is higher, but now the prospect trusts in your knowledge.

EBM Stage 5 – (Maximum risk / Identity-Based Trust). At this stage you have established trust, a level of rapport and the prospect is prime to now transition into a client... You are at a stage where the prospect knows you, likes you and trusts you. Through a sales call or meeting, your job is to now find out the prospect's problem, or need matches the promise of what your service or product offers. If the perceived value of what you offer outweighs them staying where they are or better yet, using the services or products of a competitor, they are now prime to become a customer.

Understanding these five stages will ensure you have these key areas covered when it comes to preparing EBM content that will put the right message in front of your leads and prospects at the right time.

BUT! There are exceptions to the rules. The stages act as a guide, and these guidelines can be blurred or even skipped. What matters most is knowing that when prospects come across your marketing message, content and advertising, you're ready for the top three most desired levels in the Customer Buying Pyramid.

An example of EBM content and how the stages work together

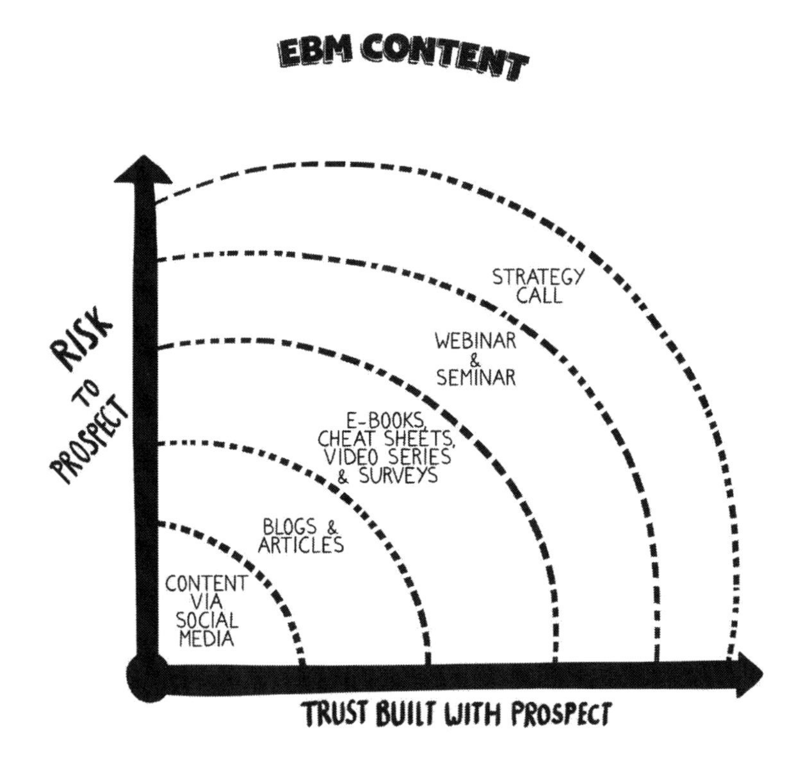

Below are the five Types of Content You Can Create, which directly link to the five levels of EBM, so you can clearly understand what is needed and how you can market your message best.

EBM Stage 1 – Content On Social Media (Native Platforms)

Create and post a blog article, or video, live stream directly to the social media platforms that your audience currently uses. If you're targeting clients offline, you can send direct mail to their physical address. Your content should not require your lead to change the environment where they reside. No external clicking onto another website or application. EBM Stage 1 is all about keeping your audience comfortable, yet providing enough value and difference so much, so they pay ATTENTION to the content you're sharing.

EBM Stage 2 – Blogs & Freely Available Content

If you've not created a blog yet, a blog is simply a series of articles that you create to offer your readers relevant content that helps them within your niche. There are many different styles of blog articles, ranging from professional, first person, third person, factual, fictional, non-fictional, your true personality, your professional alter ego and so on. Remember, you choose your story angle.

There is no right or wrong way, but when you come from a place of helping people with their problems, you can structure your blog articles in a way that uses the 5 stages of the EBM formula, so that you increase trust and scale risk with your readers, whether they are simply casual or regular readers.

There are many successful businesses online that simply run as a blog. They gain trust, increase readership and off the back of great content, they market and promote many different types of products to their captive audience. There are many coaches who set up a blog and their articles are super professional, but they lack any type of personality. It makes for an easy read that captures the logic of a readers mind but lacks any potency when it comes to engaging the readers emotions.

Video

Without going overboard, video is a major force in your marketing arsenal. There are so many stats that prove its ability to capture the attention of your audience and keep them engaged longer.

Your strategy and tactics must include video if you wish to capitalise on the potential engagement, attention, and ability to be omnipresent (appear to be everywhere) in the eyes and ears of your audience. Short videos up to 2 minutes, medium videos 2-20 minutes and longer videos 20 minutes plus. The video types include: how to's, explainers, animation, demo's, video sales letters, sideways sales letters, opt-in page, live streams, off the cuff audience engagement, music, parody, viral, company intro, webinars and much more…

Current Video Statistics;

- Video drives a 157% increase in organic traffic from Search Engine Results Pages.
- Videos up to 2 minutes long get the most engagement.
- 85% of Facebook videos are watched without sound.
- Video on a landing page can increase conversions by 80% or more.
- The average user spends 88% more time on a website with video.

* http://www.wordstream.com/blog/ws/2017/03/08/video-marketing-statistics

* https://wistia.com/blog/video-time-on-page

There are many benefits to the results you will achieve with video, and if being in front of the camera worries you, you can either choose to get uncomfortable or lose marketing reach for your campaigns. Consider recording videos with you as the main person in front of camera. Ask your team members who are a good fit for video. Hire actors (reasonably priced freelancers). You can have animation videos which removes the need for somebody to be on screen and simply add a voiceover. There are also webinar style videos (where you have a power point presentation, with your voice narrating the content).

The best approach to your videos will come down to your research and looking at the chosen tactics you use to target potential leads.

Podcast

A podcast is a recorded show in audio format and it's is made available on key platforms like iTunes (Apple store). It's like having your own show on a major radio station. For many people who like to listen and learn, it's a great way to get your content into the ears and minds of your target audience. Whether people listen on the go, during their commute, the gym, whilst they're cooking or simply as background learning, it serves your audience on their terms and at their convenience.

When I launched my first podcast, the idea was to create a platform that my co-host and I could use to build our legacy, forge meaningful relationships with "A" Players and make something of ourselves. It worked because we won awards, are associated with multi-millionaires and are invited to work with them.

In nine short months, we were crowned the UK's Best Business Podcast in 2015. It taught me the importance of focusing on the community or tribe you choose to build and harness. They are the oil in the engine that keeps the vehicle moving. Whilst we drive and direct its movement.

Having a podcast takes dedication like all marketing activities, so it pays to research your market, know what your customers want and deliver it to them. Having a podcast is pretty straightforward to setup, and there are apps that allow you to record straight from your smartphone, so you don't have the need a professional microphone, headphones or expensive recording equipment. However, it does help if you choose to take the quality to the next level.

The key steps to setting up a podcast.

1. Decide if you will interview people or simply deliver your own content or both.

2. Build up a series of 10 episodes before you launch so you're ready to give lots of value upfront.
3. Decide how often you will publish your episodes.
4. Create a content calendar of episodes for your show.
5. Edit your audio episodes to remove ums and arrs. (outsource if needed)
6. Upload each episode onto a media host like Libsyn, Spreaker or Soundcloud.
7. Publish your podcast to iTunes & Stitcher.
8. Publish each episode to your website too.
9. Market each episode to your audience on the relevant social media platforms.
10. Stick to it for at least a year to build up great content and commitment to your audience.

Testimonials & Case Studies

In EBM stage 2, testimonials can be used in a variety of ways and cross the boundaries of all EBM stages because they contain content relevant to influence your prospects and persuade them to buy from you. They trigger the desires of your prospect by them wanting what you have. Whether text or video, testimonials play a big part in showing what you can do and why you're worth as much as you are.

With technology and using familiar visual screen-shots or print screens of testimonials received on Facebook, LinkedIn, Amazon, Yelp, TripAdvisor, Yellow Pages, etc, they further enhance your social proof with prospective clients when used on web pages, sales letters and in videos, etc.

Here is a testimonial template I use with clients;

1) Intro - who you are, what do you do, and how did we meet?
2) Problem - what was the major problem/s and circumstances before you started working with us?

3) Story - how did you feel and what did you try before that didn't work? Elaborate on it.
4) Results - how do you feel now? What changes did we help you make and what is different compared to before you worked with us.
5) Emotion - how do you FEEL about where life is heading and what's going to be different going forward?
6) Sum up - sum up the program you've done, and what it could do for others. Do it in one sentence.

Case Studies are similar to testimonials but have a slightly different structure. They show what your customers have to say about you, your product or service.

A simple case-study structure: (1) Need/Problem (current situation) (2) Approach (method/solution used) (3) Impact (result achieved) and(4) Client Testimonial. With this outlined for a prospect who is going through a similar problem, the case-study represents hope and knowing that you've done it for someone else, there's a good chance they will have the same positive result too.

Testimonials and Case studies are powerful ways to add emotion and certainty in persuading prospects about your ability and the types of results you can help them achieve.

Press Releases

Press releases can act as a great way to blow your own trumpet and make people aware of something noteworthy you've done. Press release articles can be featured on various mediums such as local press, regional, national offline or online on influencer or big audience websites. It can act as an endorsement for being associated with the organisation publishing your press release and let your potential leads know you are worth paying attention to. Even at the smallest level, you have the validation of being branded by association as you're linked to the publisher of your article.

Press releases are great tools for positioning. Being published with the right company in the right market can significantly impact your presence in a place where you're not really known or where you wish to establish a stronger foothold for your business or an upcoming campaign.

EBM Stage 3 – Lead Magnets, Checklists, Guides, Video Series & Ebooks

By using the benefits of EBM Stages 1 and 2, you're now "in the game" when it comes to your prospect. They now know you and like you and now at the stage where they will demonstrate they are willing to trust you. At this moment, they're not ready to buy from you, but that's coming. They are willing and possibly wanting the next thing you have to offer, which acts as a follow up to content you published in Stages 1 and 2.

You have their interest and peaked their desire; now emotions are part of the equation. Now you want to exchange another piece of higher value content, but this time you can ask for an email, name, phone number and possibly more.

This is usually done through an opt-in page, free offer on an advert (online or printed press/letter, etc) or a phone call. The key difference here is that the lead is willing to risk giving you their contact details knowing that they will be given access to some form of checklist, guide, report, video or Ebook. The perceived value in their eyes is worth it.

At EBM Stage 3, you now have a LEAD – someone you can have two-way communication with.

EBM Stage 4 – Webinars & Seminars

Now that we are at EBM Stage 4, it's time to turn up the trust and level of risk the lead is willing to give. When a lead registers for a webinar, they are now committing time in their schedule for a 45-120 minute presentation.

If they have registered for an event or better yet paid, you essentially you have a customer. They are committing time, travel costs, and time out of their business. They are at the point where their problem must be fixed and they are actively seeking out more information than when it was less urgent or important. They are looking for the right provider (you).

Their emotions are driving them to seek a solution and they will take up your offer so long as what you offer answers their objections; you give them enough reasons to trust and an irresistible offer is made.

You are also in a unique place where you can further qualify the prospect and prepare them for your offer, closing the sale knowing you are a good fit for each other. Be mindful of maintaining your integrity in sales at this stage.

EBM Stage 5 – Sales Calls or Meetings

Stage 5 is the ultimate level in EBM because you're transitioning your *prospect* into *client* status. To recap, at Stage 1 you were in the process of hooking the attention of a would-be lead. Stage 2 you provided immense value, and the client is consumed your information, which built their trust. Stage 3, they shifted from prospect to lead and gave you their name, email, a phone number...maybe more. Stage 4, they're willing to invest time and or money with you, and you're booked into their calendar.

In EBM Stage 5, you've established trust, and the prospect knows you, likes you and trusts you. They are willing to take a risk and buy your product or invest in your service. Your final job is to answer objections with your knowledge, benefits, USP, guarantee, and testimonials, and/or case studies. When you've answered all their needs, the prospect has given you buying signals that it's time to ask for the sale and close the deal.

CHAPTER ACTION SUMMARY

What you need to put into Action

- ⦿ AUTHORity – the process or creating
    - ▪ Use positioning to build authority
    - ▪ Use storytelling to increase trust
    - ▪ Choose the hero you wish to be for your audience
    - ▪ Use storyline angles how to connect with your audience
    - ▪ Use emotions to be build trust
- ⦿ AIDA Formula (use this to motivate your prospects to become clients)
- ⦿ EBM Formula (use this to educate your prospects up to the level of wanting to become your client)

Refer to the MLMC Workbook to work on these key points.
www.moreleadsmoreclientsbook.com/resources

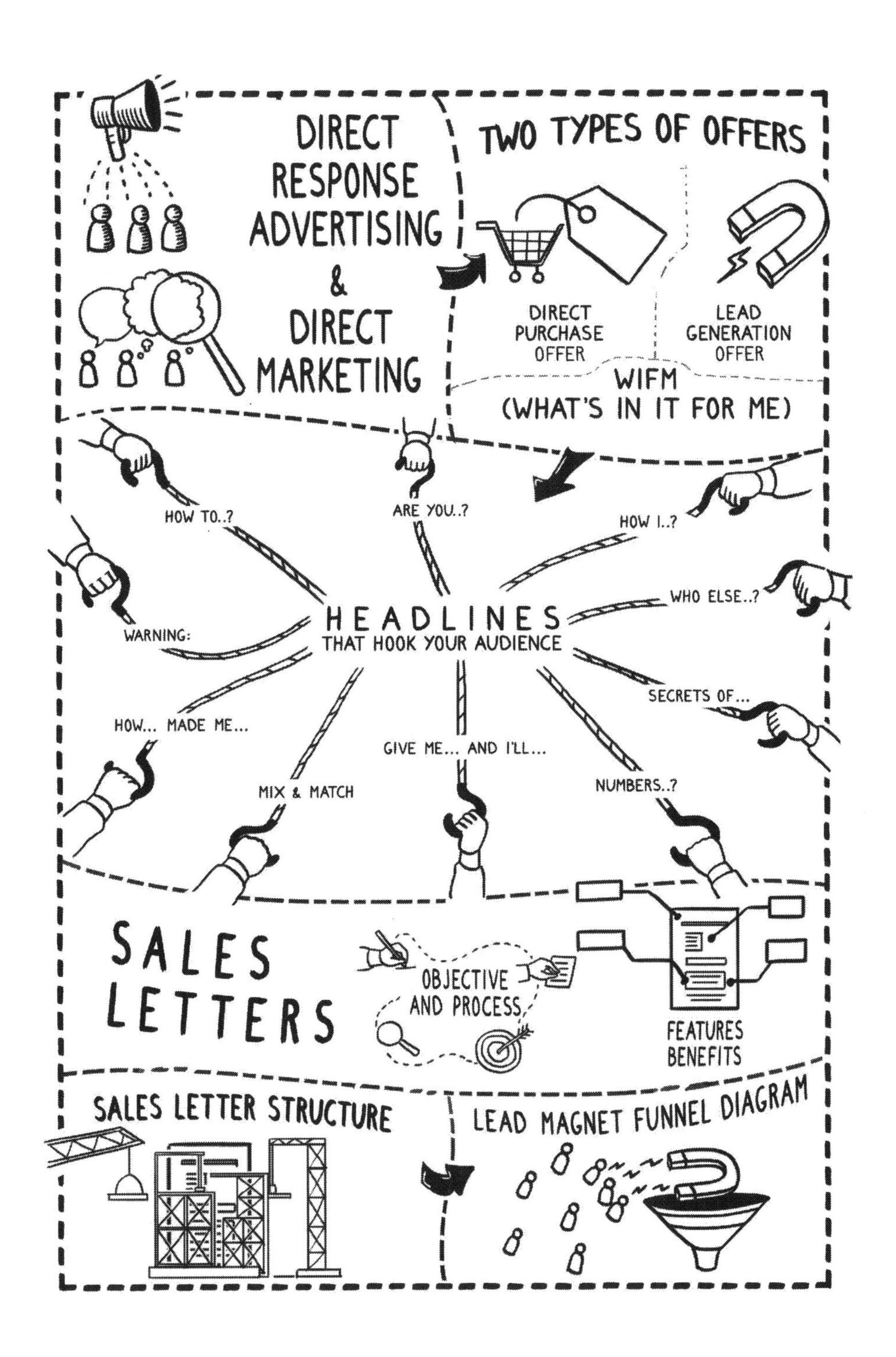

DIRECT RESPONSE ADVERTISING & DIRECT MARKETING
TWO TYPES OF OFFERS
DIRECT PURCHASE OFFER
LEAD GENERATION OFFER
WIFM (WHAT'S IN IT FOR ME)
HOW TO..?
ARE YOU..?
HOW I..?
WHO ELSE..?
WARNING:
HEADLINES THAT HOOK YOUR AUDIENCE
SECRETS OF...
HOW... MADE ME...
GIVE ME... AND I'LL...
MIX & MATCH
NUMBERS..?
SALES LETTERS
OBJECTIVE AND PROCESS
FEATURES BENEFITS
SALES LETTER STRUCTURE
LEAD MAGNET FUNNEL DIAGRAM

CHAPTER 3

Why Direct Marketing Is Critical

You may not understand the reason or strategy behind your competitors ability to invest a lot of money on their image, brand building, lead generation, and market-place presence campaigns.

You're choosing to be different as I offer information in this book. Your goal isn't to spend (waste) money to get your name out there. You're actually in the game to invest your money into advertising and marketing that offer you a simple result. **For every £1 you put in, you want** £2 back out in sales. It's that simple...

You're not supposed to emulate big companies. They're big for a reason, but remember, like you, they started small. They have invested time to start, grow, go through the ups and downs, and breaking through to getting paid. They finally reached a tipping point of size, where their presence in a market and niche grew to a size close to domination.

Many coaches fail when they try to copy the methods of a giant, who are years and into their business journey.

Your job is to sell something now, get paid and have money in the bank! Your bills aren't going to pay themselves...and the more you get paid, the more space you create in your mind to think about your next goal.

Direct Response Advertising & Direct Marketing

Direct Response Advertising is the channel where you advertise your offer.

Direct Marketing is making an offer so the responses can be tracked and measured...

Two types of offers

There are generally two types of offers that exist. An offer requesting a purchase or lead generation offer. Again, lead generation is when a person effectively opts in, registers, proverbially holds their hand up to identify themselves as having an interest in what you're offering and is open to further communication from you. Often the lead generation offer is free, but it can also be priced at a low investment amount to trigger that first buying interaction with you.

Direct Purchase Offer

The direct purchase offer is when you have an offer for a product or service. It's best to create a deadline or limited number of available spots to encourage people to take action. You may include a bonus gift or product to sweeten the deal.

Examples:

- Buy one pizza get the second half price or free.
- Fill up your car with a tank of petrol and get a free flashlight
- Get this book free and only pay for shipping
- 50% off window sale on now
- We have only 50 of these brand new heaters in stock and every one must go by the 1st December.

However, direct purchase offers have disadvantages. You're training the customer to wait for special offers before they buy, which is the wrong type of attitude to have. The other disadvantage is that you're targeting the top 3% of people who are in a position to buy now, explained in the Customer Buying Pyramid earlier, which means you will miss out on the other potential prospects (67%) who would likely buy in the near future.

Doing this makes your customers price compare you, which creates a sales culture where the urgency to buy will fortify a person's reasoning to shop around first.

Lead Generation Offer

The Lead Generation offer gives you the ability to test and measure your offers before you've committed large sums of money to roll out campaigns. They work powerfully because they can slide directly into the EBM Formula. You can build trust and scale a prospect's risk level to the point they purchase because you have created an education culture and are now considered a trusted advisor. This is known as a Lead Magnet – an offer of value that attracts a lead.

For example;

- A Marketing Coach offers a free 5-10 page guide with the promise to show how he attracted over 1000 leads without spending a penny on ads.
- A Business Coach offers a free 3-part video series to help business owners increase their revenue using a specific sales methodology.
- A Life Coach offers A free 5-part audio series with a bonus workbook to help men aged 25–50 finally break free of bad habits.

This approach allows you to save your money and not lose it by investing in a full marketing campaign. You can test your lead generation offer and see how your market responds. You can also test subtle changes in the Call To Action (CTA) to see how your prospects respond to your main offer.

WIFM (What's In It For Me)

If you can't answer this for your prospect, your advertising will fail because your prospects won't bother to look at your ad, let alone respond to it.

To truly master the art of getting leads to respond and raise their hand, you must show what's in it for them. It's not a matter of showing your product or service, and then hope they will come and buy it. Your job is to create a compelling, irresistible offer that shows a customer what's in it for them by solving their problem. You give them an opportunity to either buy from your direct offer or to opt into your lead generation offer that delivers value.

Why Understanding Threshold Resistance Is Important

A. Alfred Taubman was one of America's most successful entrepreneurs. His fascinating life and career were chronicled in his best-selling business memoir, *Threshold Resistance: The Extraordinary Career of a Retailing Pioneer*. Threshold resistance – a phrase he coined to describe the psychological and physical barriers that keep a shopper from entering a store."

Offers will fall into one of two categories – High Threshold or Low Threshold.

A High Threshold offer usually requires money upfront – £97 for a discovery call or access to a webinar for £49. It requires a decision upfront and parting with money before any relationship has started. If you don't know them, you risk price/service comparison.

A Low Threshold offer is when information is offered for free in exchange for contact details, name, email, phone number, and address, etc.

Below is one of the free guides I offer using the EBM formula that establishes value in advance and start of the relationship.

With this in mind, you can choose to use a low or high threshold or even both in a marketing campaign. The key is to decipher which method works for your target market and the media you chose. Keep in mind, market forces, competitors, marketplace awareness, and sophistication will affect those choices.

Headlines That Hook Your Audience

In its simplest form, the headline is the bridge between your prospect and your product or service. Your headline's job is to get the person to read the next line of your advert, sub-headline, sales letter or the main content.

Mass Desire, How To Channel and Direct It.

The hopes, dreams, fears, emotions, and desires that already exist within your prospects are the keys to truly connecting your marketing message with your audience. It is not something you can create or own. Yet for those who find success, they learn that this must be channelled, directed, and focused into a particular product or service.

In his famed booked, *Breakthrough Advertising*, Eugene Swartzbreaks this down further for the purposes of keeping it simple. He describes "mass desire" as the public circulation of a private want that comes in two categories.

1. **Permanent Forces** – Mass Instinct. For example, the desire of women to be attractive or men to be masculine. The desire never really fades. Therefore, the message must be distinguishable compared to others that have been there before. It must shift the fulfilment of desire from one product to the new one being offered. Another example may be mass technological problems. Poor performing online ads or confusing marketing automation. Again, the message must shift fulfilment of desire from one product to the next.
2. **The Forces of Change** – Usually the beginning of change in the market, technology, or a trend. It's being aware of new innovative trends that will sweep the market and being at the front of the innovation bell curve. Knowing when early adopters have jumped on a trend andyou are able to capitalize on the bigger share of the early majority and late majority. Sensing when to shift from one benefit angle to the next continually at the front being first.

How to channel Mass Desire

1. Choose the most powerful desire that can be applied to your product.
2. Acknowledge the desire, reinforce it, and/or offer the means to satisfy it in a single statement in the headline of your messages.
3. Then, take the benefits of what your product or service offers and show your prospect how it inevitably satisfies their desire.

Example Headlines

Knowing what your headline objective is, let's look at some examples taken from successful books, advertisements, sales letters, emails, and research sources. Use these examples to help create your own headline ideas.

How to..?

This opener allows you to use a straight benefit for your reader. It's simple, yet very powerful because it instantly suggests a solution.

- How To Win Friends and Influence People.
- How To Stand Out In Business And Win More Clients
- This Breakthrough Book Will Show You How To Build A Business From "Square One" Into A 6 Figure+ Asset...

How I..?

Similar to How To but a little more personal. It all comes down to the strength of the benefit used in the headline.

- How I Stumbled Across A Marketing Technique That Unlocked A Waterfall Of New Leads.
- Here's How I Use Relationships To Get On More Stages As A Speaker.
- How I Turned $10,000 Into Over $50,000 In Three Months

How… Made Me…

Similar to How I, and shows you're willing to share a discovery

- How a Little Known Webinar Secret Made Me £23k in 23 days.
- How a 3 step Sales Process Landed Me a £150k Client Contract
- How a "Fool Stunt" Made Me a Star Salesman

Numbers..?

Numbers are a good because they get the reader to think.

- 2 little Known Secrets Coaches Can Use To Unlock A Stream Of Leads
- 3 Questions That Will Determine Whether You Have A PROFITABLECoaching Or Consulting Business!
- 5 Tools Business Owners Can Use to Radically Change Their Marketing Results

Who Else..?

This implies something that is commonly known yet the reader doesn't. Curiosity and the fear of missing out.

- Who Else Wants to Finally Meet The Man Of Their Dreams?
- Why In The World Would You Want To Read This Article Any Further… Knowing It Might Cost You £3997 At The Very Least?
- Who Else Wants To Make Big Money In Electronics?

Are you..?

The question opener gains attention by challenging and provoking the reader.

- Are Your Discovery Calls Boring Your Prospects To Death?
- Are You Prepared For The Next Wave Of Increases In Facebook Advertising Costs?
- How Much Are You Worth?

Secrets of…

Secrets, truths and so on, creates curiosity in the reader.

- Secrets of a Million, Dollar Coach
- The Truth About Confidence for Coaches
- This Fantastic Secret Turned My Life Around And Made Me Rich... Now You Can Use It Too, Without A Penny's Risk.

Warning…

Drama, interruption of the daily norms, this headline gets right to the core of fear.

- Warning: You Probably Can't Do It Without My Help!
- Stop! Don't Chase Another Client, Use The V3 Method And Have Them Chase You!
- Stop Dreaming And Start Making Money

Give me… and I'll…

This structure implies a promise around a sales message for your product or service.

- Give Me 30 Minutes Of Your Time, And I'll Turn That Into £30k In The Next 3 Months
- Let Us Help You Fill Your Coaching Programs Faster
- Give Me 5 Days, and I'll Give You A Magnetic Personality...Let Me Prove It - Free

Mix & Match...

This is where you test and let the results show you what's working.

- Revealing... The Business Owners Deepest Darkest Fears!
- The UGLY Truth About Coaches Who are NLP Qualified
- How a 10 Year Old Boy Used A Question To Uncover A Marketing Blueprint For Home Improvement Companies

Taking this one step further can really solidify your headline into being a winner by introducing a theme. For example:add a shock effect, curiosity, straight benefit, something bizarre, play on words and quotes, a contrast, a play on a book and movie title, use tv / movie characters, challenge the norm or dogma (common belief), authority and proof, seasonal (Christmas, Valentines etc) and finally test a mix and match of these themes and see which generate the best results.

Sales Letters

You're in the game of making money. Your business was created to make a difference and give you the freedom to do what you wanted and be your own boss. But without cash coming in, you have a hobby at best.I'm not here to burst your bubble, this book has been created to expand your mind, increase your knowledge and give you a solid game plan to be a success – and that means making money.

Many coaches believe the best route to their success is creating content that never actually directs the viewer or reader to buy anything.

You know what I'm talking about, "Oh that was a useful article" or "that video was really helpful."

But the biggest mistake I regularly see is no call to action (CTA) ever. Coaches have somehow become over concerned with creating content that makes them look good, but never actually present a real sales call to action.

This is why the Sales Letter is paramount to understanding what you will ultimately market and promote as you build your business. If you've created content – blogs, articles, magazine articles, technical writing, you know how to express yourself in simple language. You know how to write words that inform, pull on people's emotions, intellect, and entertains. But faced with selling (often the dirty word for many business owners), r convincing the reader (the prospect) to buy your product is a worthy and noble pursuit that you must embrace.

Readers Digest

One of my first experiences of sales letters was from the published version of the Readers digest in the UK. Back in the 90's, for me, it was all about the competitions that came through the door. Chances to win holidays and money, especially when money wasn't in big supply. I lived in hope that I may be one of the lucky ones. As you probably guessed, I never won anything, but it gave me exposure to more and more offers. I remember buying one of those offers, a world atlas in the shape of an A4 book with lots of interesting stuff a 14-year-old like me would find exciting – I'm sure I still have that book somewhere. But the point is this... The sales letter spoke to me, the offer gripped me, and I took action and bought it...

The history of sales letters date back hundreds of years, and the technique has always been pretty much the same. Identify a niche, hook with a headline on how you fix a problem, insert a story of intrigue, explain your understanding of the problem, offer a solution, show some benefits and then present an offer and way for the prospect to buy.

Sales Letter Objective and Process

One of the first steps in writing copy that sells is to write about the benefits. A benefit is what the product does, and it's what the end user of the product or service gains as a result of the feature. A feature is a descriptive fact about a product or service.

You use benefits to overcome your reader's reasons not to buy. Below are some reasons why your prospects may choose not to buy from you.

1. "You don't understand my problem."
2. "How do I know you're qualified?"
3. "I don't believe you."
4. "I don't need it right now."
5. "It won't work for me."
6. "What happens if I don't like it?"
7. "I can't afford it."

The best way to combat these reasons is to differentiate between features and benefits. Create a feature and benefit table (similar to the one below) to highlight the differences for easy comparison. These benefits should then be used as sales points in your copy.

Features	***Benefits***
A Marketing Funnel allows you to link a series of web pages together in sequential order, making a customer's journey to your offer simple.	A Marketing funnel allows you to build an automated approach to answering your prospects biggest problem that will lead to increased sales and leverage of your marketing team's resources.

Features	***Benefits***
High-protein Greek yogurt.	Enjoy a powerful, delicious yogurt that keeps you on the go throughout the day.
State-of-the-art hosting software that can handle multiple core structures of data.	You can be confident your site won't go down when your latest product offering goes viral.
We offer over 350 different online courses.	Advance your career by accessing a comprehensive range of training courses to suit your distinct needs.
An expert in social media management.	Your business will grow on autopilot with my blueprint for managing social media.
Expert guidance to help you reach your short and long-term goals.	Be the best you can be and achieve your full potential without feeling weighed down by life's challenges.
In the ELEVATION program, there are over 100 marketing resources and assets designed specifically for coaches.	Your marketing campaigns will start off at an advantage, with the easy to follow templates, so your business grows successfully without overwhelm holding you back.
As part of the ELEVATION program, you receive 1-on-1 coaching.	Create your best marketing campaigns and achieve the full potential of your goals without being frustrated by a weak marketing strategy.
Experts at helping Coaches create 6 – 7 figure marketing results	Your business will enjoy a clear outlook and path towards marketing success that results in bigger and stable 6 – 7 figure growth.

The Motivation Formula

Here's a formula that can be used with the benefits you've created to increase motivation of a prospect taking up your offer. Remember **AIDA?** The copy must gain the reader's Attention, Interest, Desire and then ask the reader to take Action that will lead to a sale.

The aim is for you to achieve the desired objective of motivating your reader (prospect) to act. My "go-to" is AIDA, and I recommend you use it too.

Why People Might Buy

Below is a list of why people might buy your product / service. Use this insight and tie these into your benefits, so you're clear on what can be used to write your copy. It's all about helping your reader understand how your product / service will help to increase their status.

• To be liked	• To be distinctive
• To be appreciated	• To be happy
• To be right	• To have fun
• To feel important	• To gain knowledge
• To make money	• To be healthy
• To save money	• To gratify curiosity
• To save time	• For convenience
• To make work easier	• Out of fear
• To be secure	• Out of greed
• To be attractive	• Out of guilt
• To be sexy	
• To be comfortable	

With your features, benefits, and reasons why defined, use the following list as an approach for preparation in creating and structuring your sales letter.

1. **Prospect Specific Research** (Part of Your Market Research) – Do you know what their interests, desires, frustrations, fears, thoughts, feelings and experiences related to what you're trying to sell are? What keeps them up at night? What eats away at them consciously and sub-consciously? What do they say to themselves when no-one is around? What is their dominant resident emotion?
2. **Write** – Pour all of your thoughts and knowledge out into the copy. Write to get paid not for applause.
3. **Let It Marinate** – Walk away for a few hours or days, then come back to it.
4. **Read Aloud** – Read it aloud. Does it flow? Do you have that conversational feel or are you tripping over words or getting tongue twisted?
5. **Aggressive Edit** – Come at it with a fresh pair of eyes. You will see things that don't make sense, or where you can say something in less words, reduction to the point where it will reads without compromising the message.
6. **Get Second Opinions** – Ask a colleague or someone who can give you an unbiased review. You don't want someone complimenting you only to inflate your ego. This won't help you get what is needed to generate good results.
7. **Edit Again** – Go back in based on the opinions, feedback and any new ideas that have come to you.
8. **Bring It To Life** – Graphics, Imagery and cosmetic visuals
9. **Test** – Get out to your market, until it's in front of people you won't actually know how good it is, nor will you know the numbers that it can help you to generate.

Sales Letter Structure

You don't have to be an award-winning copywriter to create effective sales letters. In fact, writing great sales letters is more of a science than an art. Even the pros use proven templates to create sales letters that get results. The following steps outline a template for writing foolproof sales letters.

1. **Attention Grabbing HEADLINE** –It's the most important part of your sales letter, and often referred to as the HOOK (using a fishing analogy, where you hook the fish with your bait). The headline's job is to get the attention of the reader, so they read the next line of your sales letter
2. **Sub Headlines** – Use these to help break up or emphasise key points of your sales letter
3. **The PROBLEM or NEED** – Identify the pain or passion the customer is experiencing. This should cover the clients' interests, desires, frustrations, fears, thoughts, feelings, and experiences related to the problem or need they're experiencing. Also, that you understand and present empathy.
4. **AGITATE The problem** – Be the person who keeps on picking at your customer's scab**.** The point is to move a person into action. We take on a lot of crap, punishment, stress and the rest of what business has to throw at us. Yet, all we need is the pain intensified, so we finally act and move out of that pain being comfortable or "manageable."
5. **The SOLUTION** – Present a new way of thinking, something that transforms the problem into a solution. New ideas or new methodologies that finally set the person free of those problems or serves their needs to the next level.
6. **EMOTION** – Use of visual, auditory and kinaesthetic words. Words and phrases that sensationalise and add feelingor turn up the volume and invoke emotion whilst appealing to the intellect of a prospect. Going beyond features and showing benefits.

7. **CREDENTIALS** – Present your expertise and why you or your product/service can be trusted. State things like successful case studies, prestigious companies (or people) you have done business with, the length of time you've been in your field of expertise, conferences/events where you have spoken or important awards or recognitions, etc.
8. **SOCIAL PROOF (Testimonials)** – To build your credibility and belief present, offer testimonials from satisfied customers. Show how your solution (product or service) has helped you, others and the results it achieved. Generally, testimonials will be two-fold: transformational (old vs. new) or results driven.
9. **OWNERSHIP** – Truly make your prospect know what it feels like to own the solution. Where they begin to future project themselves into the place of owning what your offering, they smell, it, taste it, become filled with the possibilities of what it now brings in their lives.
10. **GUARANTEE** – Reverse the risk and make your offer even more irresistible. Create a guarantee to tip the offer in your prospects direction. Remember, people have a built in fear that they will be ripped off. A guarantee is a sure-fire way to dispel that fear.
11. **USP** – A Unique Selling Proposition is a great way to differentiate yourself from competitors and increase your marketplace awareness.
12. **INTERNAL REPITITION** – Getting micro commitments along the way really helps with increasing and building your readers emotions to the point where they are motivated to take action with your offer. By asking leading questions in a conversational tone, you're looking to attain a proverbial Yes from your reader.
13. **ACTION** – Present the offer and price. To get the best results and have people take action, use a sense of urgency, scarcity and ethical intimidation. For example, you only have 10 places

available because that's the maximum you can have to deliver exceptional service with the time allotted.

14. **PS (PostScript)**– This is where you answer any final objections, summarise and remind them of your offer. It's often overlooked and can be a key step to convince some prospects into taking up your offer. You are not limited to just one. Use several if needed.

Example Sales Letters

Attention Grabbing HEADLINE	This Exclusive Programme Is Only For Business and Life CoachesStuck with Mediocre Results, Seeking Real Answers To Marketing Success. **"Puts Marketing On Auto-Pilot** **So You Can Finally Live Your Dreams"**
Sub Headline	Exciting New, but already proven programme causes qualified prospects to chase you down! *Sunday 10:23 am*
The PROBLEM or NEED	Dear Friend, Would you like a predictable flow of high-calibre prospects call YOU and working hard to convince you to accept them? You-know… *Dream prospects who already know what your opportunity is all about?* Getting prospects to call YOU is easy… If you know the best kept marketing secret…
AGITATE The problem	Maybe you have found that marketing is getting tougher and more expensive. You have to create so much, build a predictable marketing system and really be different from the masses of competitors who exist in your market. Although it's possible that you may be in that happy minority already having great marketing results. But you're still not where you want to be. Perhaps sick of working 50+ hour weeks keeping things running.

	You see, success at getting plenty of qualified prospects has a lot more to do with understanding marketing strategy and little to do with the latest tactic or trending social media tool. Whether you're a new or established business owner sitting under the 6-figure mark, you will never talk to anyone again who hasn't qualified themselves to your standards first! The top 1% of Coaches who've made it, your competitors, use this marketing strategy that has until now evaded you.
The SOLUTION + EMOTION + INTERNAL REPITITION + OWNERSHIP	The truth is... building a multi-6 or 7 figure business without an "in-the-know" someone, who is there to guide you, is not easy. Building a real business, at times, is not easy. And a successful "mentor" or"coach" can make it easier. And that's why I'm here to help...I want to show you the easy way - the right way to Build it... Market It... And Set It Up, so you work less and make more. Now there's a new, 100% measurable replacement for old-fashioned Business Marketing! Imagine how different life would be in you only ever talked to prospects who called you, those who looked at you as the authority in your market and were eagerly anticipating your opportunity (product or service). Do you think you'd feel more successful? That you'd be able to finally show people your full potential? That you'd hear people talking about you in a positive way and that life would appear brighter? This is no pipedream! Look - if you're serious about building a business that will set you free - both financially and in time - you need to take a careful look at becoming the newest member of my "Vortex Mastermind Programme". My "Vortex Mastermind Programme" will give you the Step-By-Step roadmap you need to Market a Business that can bring you the Freedom, Prosperity, and Abundance You Truly Deserve...

	Whilein the programme, you have access to our exclusive membership academy with 8 power modules, carefully crafted marketing & sales training, copy & paste scripts, how to's, videos, audio, pdf's, templates and much more. During the 12 months break-through period we meet once every 90 days for an intensive workshop where you have direct access to my team and I, as we help you build a marketing system, take care of the marketing strategy, technology integration and correct any past bad experiences you've had with marketing.
CREDENTIALS	In my first Coaching Group, there were 30 clients. After implementing what they learned (precisely what you're going to learn), and after just a few short months... Collectively they now have a marketing system that brought in leads, prospects, and real cash.
SOCIAL PROOF (Testimonials)	Take Pin Binning, "When I first came to Leon, I ran a normal solo-preneur business, just me working 60+ hours a week. Then after going through the Vortex Programme, I now have 19 other people and my income is better than ever. From one marketing strategy, I have now pulled in over £50,000 in four months." Christy Rutherford, "My main problem was I wasn't talking to my market and my messaging wasn't right. Now, I've hit a milestone moment, I've just sold my first high-value programme at $3997. Thank you!" Nate Lindquist, "I generated over $768k of coaching sales in 4 months with Leon's support. He is the real deal." These are just a smidgen of the testimonials that have been flooding into my office since launching my vortex coaching program. It's simply proof-positive that if these people can do it, so can you. In fact, you have my word that you can do it!

GUARANTEE	Here's my 30-day guarantee…Apply today, and once accepted. Go through all the training, join all the coaching calls, use all the resources, take action & implement the work and if for any reason you are not happy, just let me know and I will give you all your money back.
USP	Imagine removing all of the stumbling blocks you're facing, finally creating a marketing system that allows you to earn more, serve more clients and give you the lifestyle you've set your sights on… Well, this is it.
ACTION + Scarcity + Motivating Action	Here's How You Can Get Phenomenal Results For Your Business Right Now Once You Apply To Enrol On The Vortex Mastermind Programme. Due to the "in-the-trenches hands-on approach," I am very particular about the clients we take on, which means we can only work with ten business owners. So if you're ready to crack the marketing secret and increase your business results, you'll have to complete an application, which will be reviewed personally by me. Only if you're approved at that stage will you be invited for a phone call interview. Thanks for reading and I look forward to seeing you on the programme. Leon Streete.
PS	PS - The Vortex Mastermind will undoubtedly bridge your knowledge and earning gap plus take you into the inner circle of 6-7 figure earners. If you've skipped to the end – here's the offer – finally own a predictable and proven system to grow your business with marketing, apply here: www.businessownerelevation.com/vortex-opportunity-application/ PPS –When you join you have immediate access to 4 business boosting bonuses. 1 - Free monthly coaching training for 12 months.

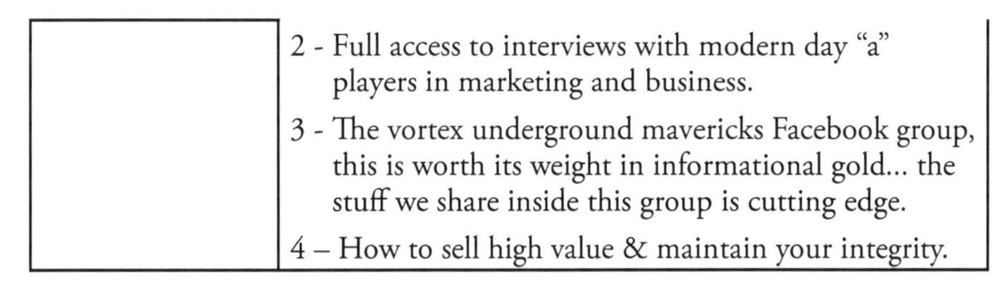

2 - Full access to interviews with modern day "a" players in marketing and business.

3 - The vortex underground mavericks Facebook group, this is worth its weight in informational gold... the stuff we share inside this group is cutting edge.

4 – How to sell high value & maintain your integrity.

Here are three examples of how I've used the sales letter template in funnels and on LinkedIn and Facebook;

- Resources - www.moreleadsmoreclientsbook.com/resources

Now that you've crafted your sales letter the next step is to get it in front of your prospects. You can deliver the sales letter in many formats, direct mail (printed onto paper and posted), on a web page, or in other formats like **Webinars***which are explored later on in chapter 7.*

Funnels Using Lead Magnets

A lead magnet is a Lead generation offer – discussed earlier with the two types of offers. It can be a PDF, printed checklist, guide, cheat sheet, copy of a presentation, a video you record of yourself on your phone, a video recording of some type of teaching on your computer screen (webinar). You demonstrate what your lead needs to know and include the right offer as the call-to-action to move your lead to the next stage of your marketing funnel.

Note: Often I come across many Coaches who divulge and go into heavily teaching, meaning they give away the HOW which can cause your lead (reader/viewer) to think "I will take this knowledge and try it out myself." This is not easy to do, and it is a matter of practice and knowing the right structure to achieve the balance of providing value and gaining your readers' curiosity to take the next step urgently or with enough belief of what will happen next as a positive outcome for them.

Putting together your Lead Magnet Funnel, will need to include a little structure to be in a position to advertise it. You will need to have:

- **Funnel Pages** – The Opt-In Page - a person enters their name/ email. Thank You Page - where after opting in, you thank the lead for downloading your content piece.
- **Email Automation** – A software you use to save the lead's name/ email. Usually, your email marketing provider will have some form of automation feature that allows you to trigger a series of automated Soap Opera Sequence (SOS) Emails.
- **Email Marketing** – Usually the same software that triggers the automation, you use to prepare a series of SOS emails (five or more). Your first email would normally include a download link for the lead magnet they opted in for; then you follow that up with email that continue to build a relationship and trust with the lead.

For example:

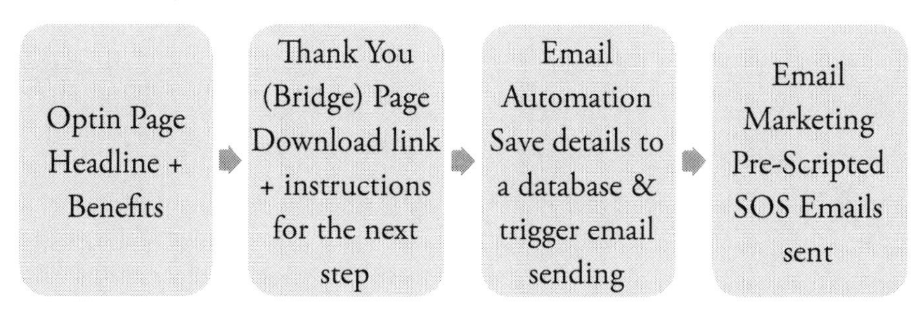

In Chapter 5, we break down marketing and lead magnet funnels more with some examples and scripts.

CHAPTER ACTION SUMMARY

What you need to put into Action

- ◉ Understand Direct Response Advertising & Direct Marketing
- ◉ Know the difference between the two types of offers
    - Create Lead Generation Offers that show your clients what's in it for them
    - Channel and direct mass desire in your niche
    - Use headlines as a way to HOOK your audience
    - Create a Sales Letter and use the Sales Letter structure for your product / service
    - Implement a lead magnet funnel to create a marketing system that can be used over and over

Refer to the MLMC Workbook to work on these key points.
www.moreleadsmoreclientsbook.com/resources

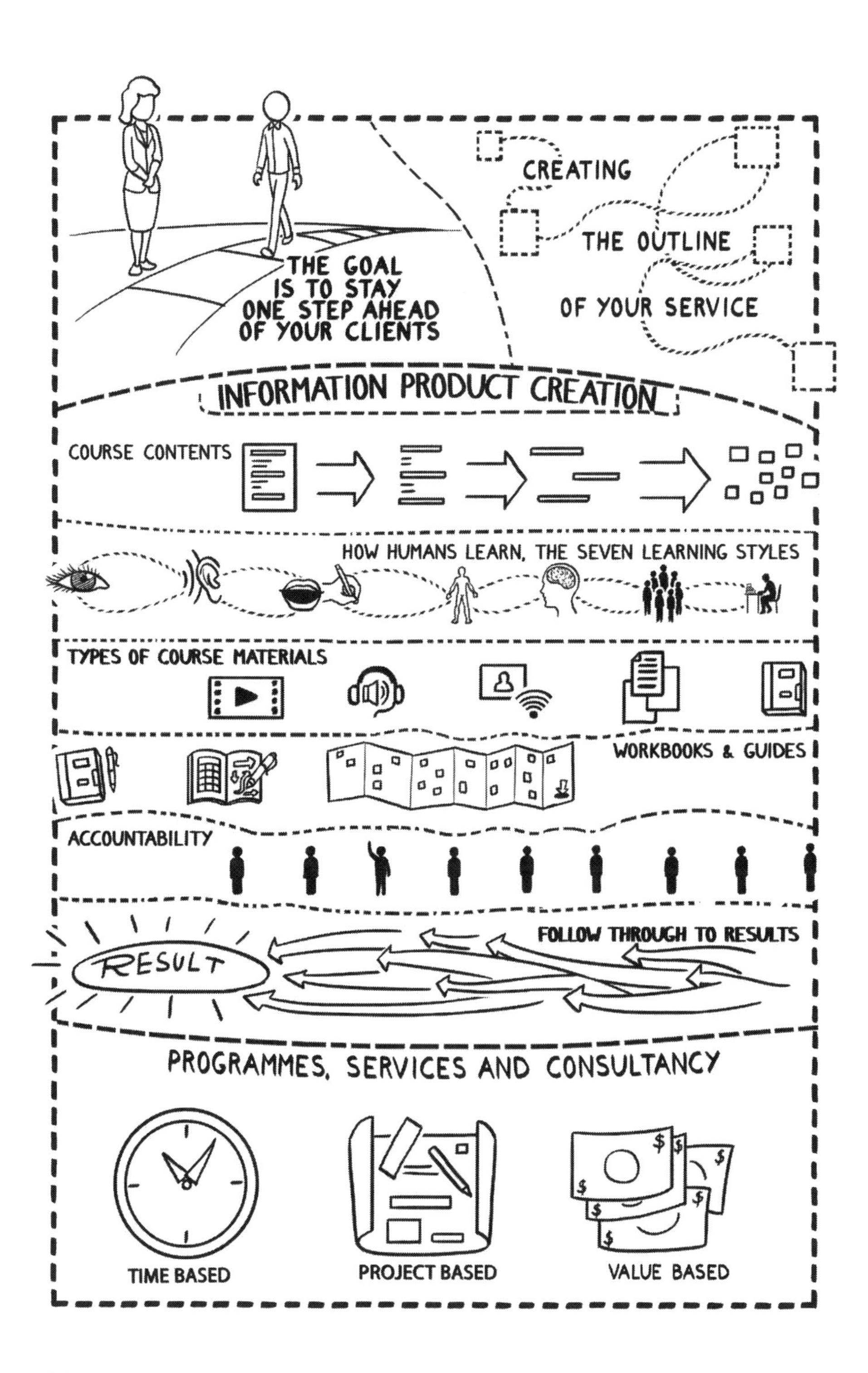
CREATING
THE OUTLINE
OF YOUR SERVICE
THE GOAL
IS TO STAY
ONE STEP AHEAD
OF YOUR CLIENTS
INFORMATION PRODUCT CREATION
COURSE CONTENTS
HOW HUMANS LEARN, THE SEVEN LEARNING STYLES
TYPES OF COURSE MATERIALS
WORKBOOKS & GUIDES
ACCOUNTABILITY
FOLLOW THROUGH TO RESULTS
RESULT
PROGRAMMES, SERVICES AND CONSULTANCY
TIME BASED
PROJECT BASED
VALUE BASED

CHAPTER 4

How To Create Your Products & Services

You get to choose the type of product or service you will offer, my advice is to stick to what you're skilled at. When you're starting out, never include skills you don't understand or possess. Eventually, you will understand more and increase your confidence to introduce new skills and partners.

"Whatever is important to you it's always going to be worth more to somebody else. You've just got to figure out who has a bigger need to have the problems solved than even you do. It's an opportunity for you, it's a solution to a problem for somebody else. But you have to verbalise it because they'd never realise it." Jay Abraham

Going into opportunities blindly is not a smart move, but shying away from them isn't wise either. Partnering with someone whose strengths differ from yours, but compliment what you do, can help you avoid missing out on great opportunities. If for any reason you're launching into a new business or going into a market and you're not up to the right skill level, understand you only ever have to be one step ahead of your client, so don't think for one second that you will need to be at Ph.D., Masters or Degree level in order to start.

You may involve third party team members (sub-contractors and freelancers) in certain scenarios. You will simply have to be on the ball when it comes to project managing these people unless you employ a project manager to do this – but they will have to report to you. The goal is to stay one step ahead and with a team so you will be at least two steps ahead in delivering what your client needs at full value.

Products have lots of advantages, the first being leverage of time. You create or buy them in, then offer the product based on it being replicated many times. Either through manufacturing or as a digital course made up of multi-media materials (videos, audio, and documents) that work without you being there, yet still delivers value to your clients.

What you offer as a Coach will depend on your goals and preference. If you're new, you want to get started by testing your services with a number of 1-on-1 clients, then expand and offer a group programme (1 to many). Maybe you're only interested in putting a product into your chosen market without having to physically turn up to deliver services (like an online course), so you will have more time freedom. Whatever you choose, it's your job to follow through and get results so that you can test and measure what's working and what's not.

Why have I left talking about your product and service until now?

The reality is that most businesses in my experience can sell a product or service simply because they have the right offer – they don't actually need the product to be ready now, which is why the previous chapters dive into the critical areas of strategy, research, positioning, and direct marketing.

Let me explain; 1 – if an individual decides to be coached they may not start coaching with you until a week, two weeks or in a months' time 2 – If you create an online course it may launch 4 weeks from now. The point is that in both cases the service and product can be sold ahead of them actually being ready (delivery). The approach debunks the idea of build it, and they will come, I say create an irresistible offer, get that offer to convert then go build it and deliver with integrity, value, and service.

I know for many, you may be feeling a bit twitchy, "saying oh no, it must be ready before I can sell it". But imagine, you create it – go to sell it, and nobody buys it, or if someone does – they buy it and it really hasn't been researched in the right way, and the service isn't fit for purpose.

In the upcoming sections of this chapter, I will break down two key ways that you can serve your clients. Products –digital courses accessed online and Services – delivered using online tools for communication, fulfilment (delivery) and more as 1-to-1 or 1-to-many.

Creating The Outline of your service

When it comes to putting together your product or service, you may wonder, "Where do I start?" Imagine you were about to make a cup of tea. Now think of the main steps needed for you to complete the entire task. For example:

1. Fill the kettle with water
2. Boil the water in the kettle
3. Prepare a cup for consumption
4. Add a teabag (add sugar or sweetener if wanted)
5. Pour in the boiled water
6. Add milk if required
7. Stir the water in the cup
8. Remove the tea bag
9. Serve...

The very action of going through each step is what you must do to uncover the key milestones in your product or service. Think of a book; it has a title and chapters. In this case, the title would be your service or product name and the chapters would be the main points of delivery or modules. To get started, think of and list the key points of delivery, usually 4-10. Now, write out three features and related benefits for each point.

View the example in the Workbook

www.moreleadsmoreclientsbook.com/resources

Information Product Creation

Knowing how to leverage your skills and knowledge from information products to help you achieve time leverage and your income goals is a goal for many. Even being in a position where you earn directly from delivering services is a big step when you're starting out or established, and looking at introducing new products to your current offering.

What I like about products and programmes is not only the leverage they offer, i.e., not having to be present but the speed at which you can gain direct feedback from your clients to improve your products. When you have users, they pay attention because they have invested their money and time. This allows you to improve your offer quickly so that as you scale and grow, you put more effective and customer beneficial products into your chosen market.

Let's look at how you create a course from the first steps of knowing your customers' problems and needs. First, you've identified a need or a problem that a product or programme (a mix of your time and a digital course – modules, lessons, video and documents etc.) can fix.

Check the information you received by running your survey, as discussed in chapter 1 (How To Read Your Prospects Mind) of this book.

Business Coach Survey. Many may have asked questions like, how do I grow my business, how do I overcome procrastination, how do I get out of debt and into profit, how do I increase sales, and how do I build a team that I can trust?

The answers to these questions can be packaged into some type of Business In A Box, product or programme.

Course Contents

Just like a book with chapters, think of your course or programme as the same. Break up the product into sections to make it easier to think about the key areas that will get your customers their desired result.

Going back to the 4 steps of Product, Placement, Pricing & Packaging, you have gathered the most common problems and needs of your client. Group these elements together to form your key areas (your modules") and the related lessons in each.

Welcome and Introduction

Your introduction module should set the foundation of your client's expectations. You will be introducing them to the way they need to think, and they will need to understand the rules of the game.

- How they can contact you
- Your availability
- The schedule of work and
- The key materials they will need to use first

With the welcome and introduction module set, the next series of modules will form the key areas of your course that will answer the problems and needs of your clients, based on the promise of your course. Four to eight modules are adequate. If you feel there needs to be more, that's ok. You may also want to consider amending it over time based on feedback of past participants.

In one of the courses we run, in one year it went through six updates to make it better, and I expect it to go through the same going forward. Not all courses will need updates or modifications, but if your clients ask for specific and new answers that they can't find then changes will be needed.

The Final Module of your programme should be the crescendo to your course. The climax, where you leave your clients on a high and clear on what their next steps are. Your clients will progress at different rates. Some will be happy to have gone through the course, will take some valuable lessons and know in what their next steps should be.

Others will have progressed at a slower rate, not because of you, simply because that's how it goes. They may need some extra support to finish up their work, and this can be an upsell or you might do this for free. It's your call, but I've made thousands simply offering an extension for those that needed it.

Chunk It Down

Now that you have outlined your modules, you will need to start thinking about the actual module lessons (the content). The exact teaching will come down to your knowledge, experiences, and showing people what not to do. There will be different types of content you can create, but from a planning and preparation point of view, your content will be best delivered in chunks. Using 5-20 minute videos should give your clients enough actionable content in lengths of time that are not too long. What you will find about your clients is that they will not go through every lesson. Some may skip and others my dip in here and there. However, a select few will actually view, listen, and read everything.

How Humans Learn - The Seven Learning Styles

Knowing how humans learn will be a valuable tool in knowing how your course or products should be created with your client in mind. When creating your course content, ensure you cover the 7 main learning styles of how clients consume information.

- Visual (spatial): People who prefer pictures, images, and spatial understanding.
- Aural (auditory-musical): People who prefer sound and music.
- Verbal (linguistic): People who prefer words, both in speech and writing.
- Physical (kinaesthetic): People who prefer body, hands and sense of touch.
- Logical (mathematical): People who prefer logic, reasoning, and systems.

- Social (interpersonal): People who prefer to learn in groups or with other people.
- Solitary (intrapersonal): People who prefer to work alone and use self-study.

Types of course materials

Here's a short list of training materials and length of time ranges to consider:

- One module – containing 1 – 20 lessons
- Instructional lesson videos – 3 - 20 minutes
    - Can be face to camera or screen recording (of a presentation or demonstration on your computer).
- Audio lessons – 5 - 30 minutes.
- Webinars (online seminars) 30 minutes – 2 hours
- Documents, scripts, templates – can vary from pdf's, powerpoint slides, excel to word (the length is up to you)
- Workbooks (Focus on the actions and key steps your clients need to)

Workbooks & Guides

Using workbooks in your course, programme or product is a great way in guiding your client through the key steps you wish for them to take and to learn from. A workbook can often be the cement that seals your course together and gives your client clarity on the transformation and results they're about to receive by completing your content and teachings.

They're really powerful tools within your course as they not only guide your clients, they act as assurance and gives you the opportunity to ensure your client is progressing through your course. They also allow you to track and hold your clients accountable to achieving what they intend to get out of your course.

Accountability

There are people who take up the offer of accountability and those who let their circumstances dictate and run their businesses. Some people want a carrot (the reward) dangled in front of them, whilst others prefer the stick (the force that kicks them up the butt). As the creator of your content, it's your job to find out what makes your customers tick and what gets them to take action.

Follow through To Results

When life gets in the way of your clients and dealing with their own negative voice, they may have challenges following through and completing what they invested in. As the guiding force, whether in a 1-on-1, group, digital or pdf content, you need to ensure get your clients to promise to themselves at the start they will get what they desire from your programme.

Establish the rules of the game, so they know how to work with you or use your programme. They will also know how to properly implement and complete what they signed up for.

Programmes, Services, and Consultancy

Unlike products or programmes, with consultancy, you need to be clear from the start what you will be offering. You need to have an understanding of how much time or resources you will be trading in return of being compensated by your client. Consultancy can be a well-paid experience, but it can also be poorly paid when you under-priced or have underestimated the work at hand and don't charge your worth. There are consultants being paid £25,000 a day while others get £250. What's the difference? Results and confidence. Results they've previously achieved to demonstrate their worth and confidence in their willingness to ask for a higher rate.

Types of Services

There are three types of consultancy you can offer: time, project or value based.

Time Based – Where you state an hourly or daily rate. This can be a good place to start as a consultant, and it will come down to your courage and belief of the final number you wish to charge. The time based formula: profit + labour costs + overhead = daily fee revenue

The Breakdown: Labour

Your time is money. If you plan to take home an annual salary of £200,000 and work 252 days per year (365 days, minus Sundays, Saturdays, holidays and two weeks vacation), you will pay yourself £769 per working day.

The Breakdown: Overhead

Overhead includes recurring expenses linked with running your business, such as rent, a virtual assistant, outsourcers, phone bills, professional email, insurance, and equipment. Say all of that equals £1,500 per month or £18,000 per year. Divide your annual costs by the number of working days per year. Market-research firm Kennedy Information figures most consultants spend 58% to 62% of their time working directly for their clients – 62% of those 252 days equals 161 days per year. Grand total: £112 per day.

The Breakdown: Profit Margin

By Mooney's estimates, a consultancy's profit margin averages between 15% and 25% of its total expenses. Continuing with the overhead value – 20% of £112 is £22.

Adding It All Up

Plug those numbers back into the fee formula. Your daily fee equals £769 + £112 + £22. That's £903 per day or £90 per hour for a ten-hour day. All prices shown exclude tax.

The Problem with time based pricing is that your time becomes your ceiling, you cannot work anymore than there are hours in the day. You can amend this by hiring team members, sub-contractors or freelancers to buy back your time and increase profitability.

Project Based – Estimate and quote a project based on its time and costs to be completed with all the necessary requirements considered. Take into consideration your time (number of days multiplied by your daily rate), total time and price for hiring any external team members and resources that need to be bought in (services, materials, etc). A benefit of this approach is that the client has a fixed price so long as the scope of the project stays the same. Where-as with time based pricing, any extra time on the project will incur additional costs.

The problem whether you're new or established with this type of consultancy is the potential to get the costs or budget wrong. You can combat this by looking at examples and case studies on the internet to scope and factor in all the elements needed on a project so you don't undersell your service and put yourself in a position of loss because you price to low.

Value Based – The price is based on the value you provide, the result you will help them achieve, the perceived value of your reputation and authority, and the alternatives available to the client which can include your competitors' products or services, using a workaround or taking no action at all. These factors will swing prices from low to above average.

Using value-based pricing, you can charge at a perceived value, rather than the time it takes to actually complete the project. However, to be successful with this pricing strategy, you have to know your client's business inside out, their costs (overheads, profit margin and other factors like market forces, currency fluctuations, etc), and the alternatives available to them.

The problem with value-based consultancy is knowing how to price up projects. You can be creative and include a mix of time and project-based costs to get a baseline figure, then add on fees based on your experience and reputation. Price too high or too low, and you can lose the opportunity. Do your research on a company and directly link the results of your work for them like a commission or revenue share deal. This way, you allow yourself to command higher prices.

Alan Weiss, a top expert in the field of consulting, has written about this topic extensively states, "Value, like beauty, may be in the eye of the beholder, but it's nonetheless discussable and mutually appreciated."

To get started you may feel more comfortable using the time or project based service. My recommendation is to transition quickly into the value-based approach. This will get you maximum profitability.

My final recommendation on pricing is establish your core pricing and then create an option that is at least double that price. When you offer your program to a prospective buyer, start with the higher price and then progress to your lower, normal priced programme – if they cannot afford the higher option. This technique alone has created hundreds of thousands in extra revenue just by having it as an option.

CHAPTER ACTION SUMMARY

What you need to put into Action

- Create an outline of your service
- Create an information of digital product if needed for time leverage
- Chunk it down so it's easy to consume
- Create all the related learning and supporting materials (workbook etc)
- Map out the type of service you will offer. Remember the differences of time, project and value…

Refer to the MLMC Workbook to work on these key points.

www.moreleadsmoreclientsbook.com/resources

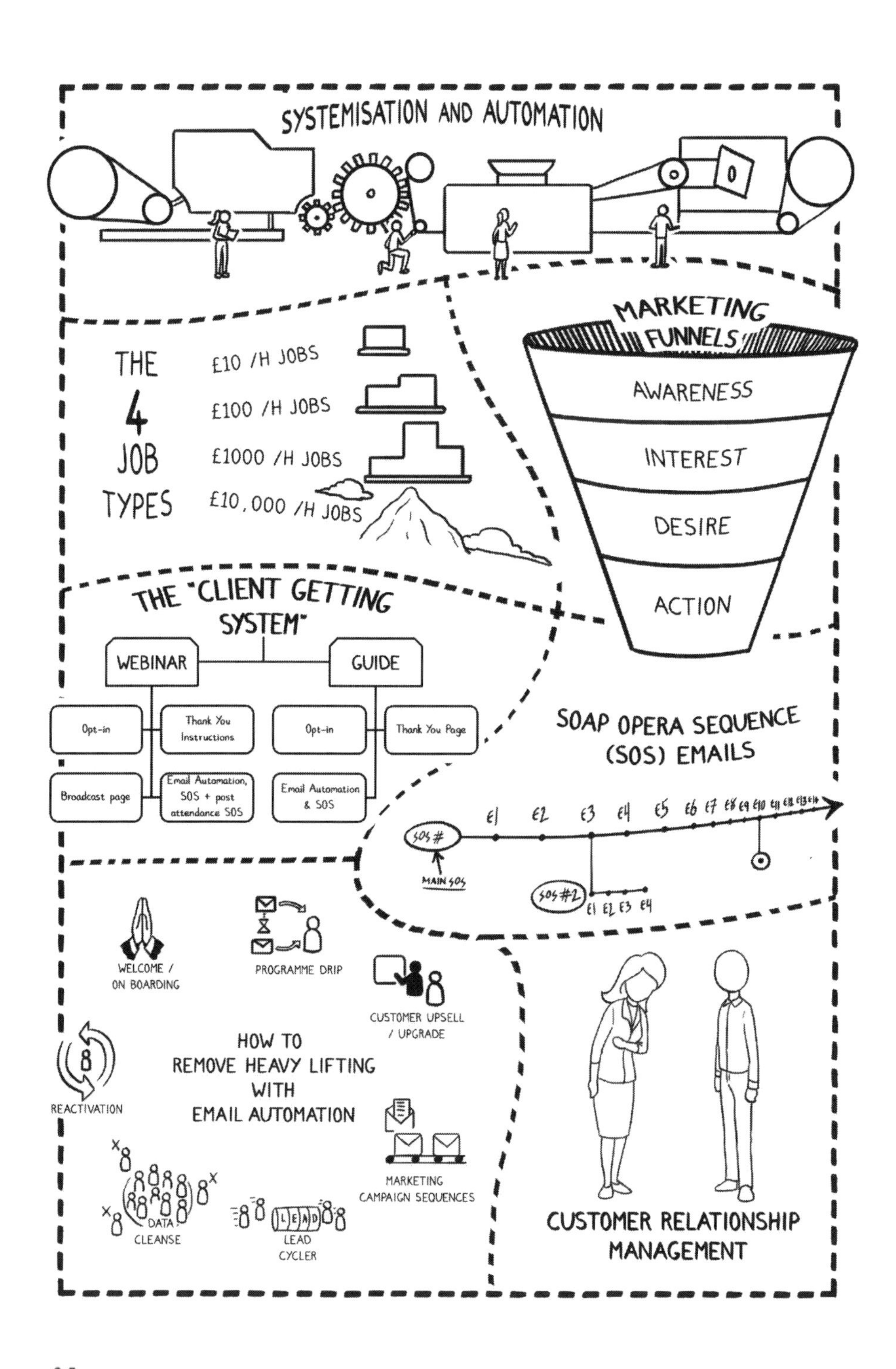

SYSTEMISATION AND AUTOMATION
THE 4 JOB TYPES
£10 /H JOBS
£100 /H JOBS
£1000 /H JOBS
£10,000 /H JOBS
MARKETING FUNNELS
AWARENESS
INTEREST
DESIRE
ACTION
THE "CLIENT GETTING SYSTEM"
WEBINAR
GUIDE
Opt-in
Thank You Instructions
Opt-in
Thank You Page
Broadcast page
Email Automation, SOS + post attendance SOS
Email Automation & SOS
SOAP OPERA SEQUENCE (SOS) EMAILS
MAIN SOS
HOW TO REMOVE HEAVY LIFTING WITH EMAIL AUTOMATION
WELCOME / ON BOARDING
PROGRAMME DRIP
CUSTOMER UPSELL / UPGRADE
REACTIVATION
MARKETING CAMPAIGN SEQUENCES
DATA CLEANSE
LEAD CYCLER
CUSTOMER RELATIONSHIP MANAGEMENT

Chapter 5

How To Create A Business That Works Without YOU!

As a business owner, *systemisation and automation* – can be scary when it comes to the technology (tech) side of your business and creating a more leveraged business. With successful marketing and sales comes systemisation – the operations manual (whether it's an actual document, videos or audio) of the key systemsin your business. When you first start out, you are the oil (the energy and passion) that keeps the engine (the business) moving. But there is only so far you can go before your time is taken up with the many different roles you have to fulfil in your business. When you get to a point where you need more resource in human power, you will need to employ team members. They can be direct employees, outsourced freelancers or subcontractors and you need to have a process in place that ensures they know how you do what you do.

Fortunately there are many great tools that can help coaches leverage their time, quality and money, but knowing what to systemise first is important.

Brad Sugars gives the best definition of a business. He said it is, "A commercial profitable organisation that works without me."

Once you get out of the infancy stage of business, you realise that it's a vehicle to where you wish to be – not a job or a life sentence. It offers you opportunity and choice, but only if it's systemised and can actually work without you while making a profit.

There are three areas you can start with systemising in your business, **marketing**, **sales** and **operations** (your service, products, accounts, HR, recruitment, legal etc).

The 4 Job Types

In his book *80/20 Sales & Marketing*, Perry Marshall stated there are generally 4 types of jobs in any business. They are:

- £10 per hour jobs –low level thinking
    - Running errands
    - Cleaning, sorting, making a drink for your team
    - Talking to unqualified prospects
    - Social media, not just mindless scrolling through your news feed
    - Building websites and marketing funnels
    - Creating graphics for social media posts and ads
    - Doing expense reports
- £100 per hour jobs–medium level thinking
    - Pay per click campaign management
    - Social media outreach
    - Helping a client fix a problem
    - Creating marketing tests & experiments
- £1000 per hour jobs – higher level thinking
    - Planning and prioritising your day
    - Writing sales copy
    - Building your sales funnel
    - Negotiating with a qualified prospect
- £10,000 per hour jobs–Top level thinking
    - Improving your Unique Selling Proposition
    - Creating new & better offers
    - Re-positioning your message and position
    - Executing "aha / light bulb" brilliant ideas

- Negotiating
- Major deals and strategic partnerships
- Public speaking
- Selling to high-value customers and groups
- Hiring team members
- Establishing values and culture

Your job is to identify the tasks in these 4 categories and begin to systemise the £10 per jobs, so you can free up more time to focus on the £100 per hour jobs. Then systemise those jobs and free up more time for £1000 & £10,000 per hour jobs. The strategy is pretty simple and common sense, just not common practice.

An example can be email replies saved as email templates, which will save you countless hours throughout a year instead of typing each one out. Also, your lead generation offers, so that you don't have to print or forward a pdf document to a prospect and then follow-up with emails each time a person requests it.

Something to note, when you begin the process of systemising remember your goal is to systemise as much as possible until human intervention is needed. You cannot systemise the job of making a drink for your client or cleaning the office, but you can systemise the procedure, how it's done, before, during and after.

With this in mind, you need to create your Operations Manual. It can be an actual document, series of documents, videos, audio (mp3 files) or a website designed with all of the mentioned content formatted for your team to easily access the systems, trainings, scripts, and templates at any time to help your business run more effectively. The operations manual should be a dynamic and organic document that grows, evolves and bends to the vision, culture and mission of your business. Whilst some things may remain the same, there are always procedures and tasks that can be improved. This type of approach will also help you bypass the limitations of thinking "that's the way it's always been done," and you can adopt that's how it's done today, but tomorrow there may be a better approach.

You should allow time to create your operations manual and build it around your sales, marketing and operations tasks. If it's a one page document, voice recording with instructions or a video you recorded today, that's okay. You've started…

Marketing Funnels

Can you go beyond the need for a website? Some people have had massive success without having any type of typical website, because the key is to provide a path for your prospects that takes them through the four stages of AIDA in an easy to follow manner.

Thanks to the advancement of technology and the speed at which they can be deployed, marketing funnels have exploded in recent years. In some cases, they have become the go to necessity in your marketing toolbox of tactics. Service providers or consultants often state you need a marketing funnel to be successful, however, it's usually before the basic steps of marketing strategy and planning have been considered to identify the needs of your customers and how they buy. This often happens with the less knowledgeable reactive coaches – not you.

Once your strategy identifies a marketing funnel is a valid tactic to use in your marketing campaign, it will open up doors to many possibilities. One of the greatest benefits is the speed of deployment and possible changes which will allow you to adapt, test and measure, and fix faster than was ever possible. You can bend to market forces and prospects' demands without breaking the bank or losing momentum.

A marketing funnel, or sales funnel refers to the journey of what a lead, then a prospect experience in becoming a client. As they progress, they experience each stage of AIDA based on the different tactics you have in place to transition them along.

The "Client Getting System"

There are two types of funnels, webinar or PDF Guide, which can both be grouped together into the "Client Getting System."

1. **An ad or promotion**
2. **Webinar or PDF Guide (strategically linked web pages connected to an email automation database)**
3. **An application or order form**
4. **A sales call & close**

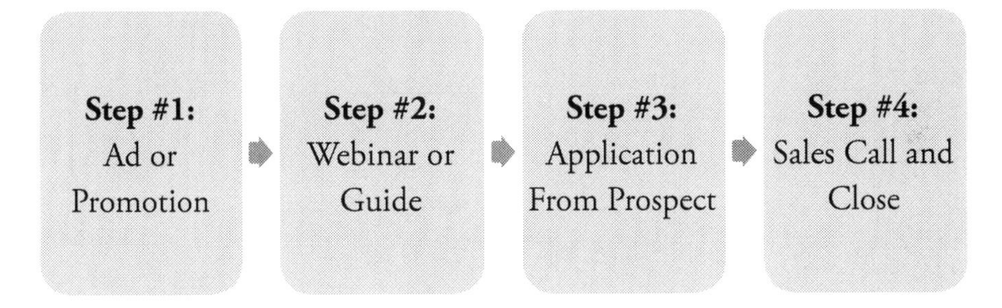

With the two types of media (webinar/guide), they offer something for the main ways your target audience will want to consume your content. People who like to watch video (webinar – Live or Pre-recorded) see and hear and others who like to read (a pdf guide).

There is a structure to follow just like the sales letter, but there is also a template style that must be used. The reason for this is that if you try to cram the equivalent of a 1-10 or more page sales letter into slides, it will be crammed with information and will not work in the way that a well-structured webinar works.

As part of the Client Getting System, there are **Soap Opera Sequence (SOS)** Emails. In each funnel, there is a trigger for sending emails, usually the opt-in or registration. SOS Emails are an episodic form of pre-scripted email, designed to be released on schedule (usually day after day) five or more emails to the subscriber. This concept was first introduced by Andre Chaperon in the early 2000's. It usually results in them getting to know you better by encouraging them through stories and open loops (cliff hangers – stories spread over multiple episodes) to build their anticipation of the follow-up email. The goal, once trust is established, is to get them to buy from you, through links placed in the emails to your order form or sales letter page.

The release schedule of these change as the emails act as a countdown to the live webinar date. After the webinar, you can easily introduce a follow up series of SOS Emails to make sure that anyone who missed the webinar or didn't take up your offer sees it again.

If you use a pre-recorded webinar, you may offer instant access to your webinar video and an SOS Email series after the initial opt-in to either encourage people who did not take up the webinar offer, or to continue to build the relationship with your email subscriber.

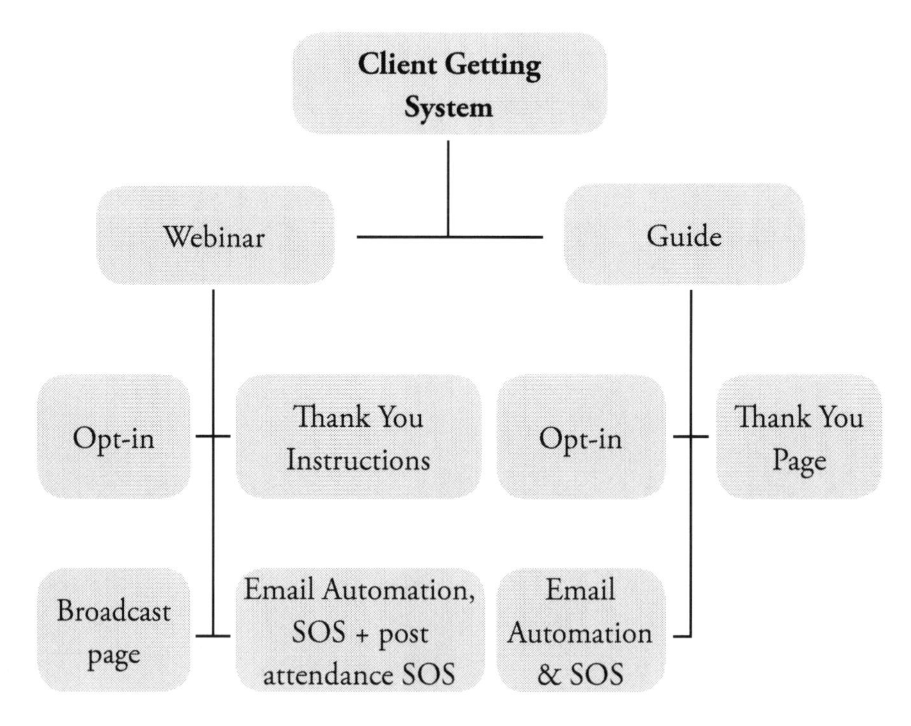

To make this step easier for you, remember to download the example email scripts in the free workbook.

www.moreleadsmoreclientsbook.com/resources

How To Remove Heavy Lifting With Email Automation

One of the really cool things, about email automation is that it comes with some super cool features and benefits even the savviest coaches don't know about. This is where your email marketing system comes into its own, from a leveraged point of view.

For example: When a new client joins your company, add a tag (#client) to their record in your email marketing/customer relationship management (CRM) software. Then, as if by magic, a welcome text (SMS) message is sent to them. Also, a sequence of welcome emails at a specific time(in their time zone), directing them to all of the relevant resources, content and the first steps to making them feel welcome. As they access the different pieces of content (they visit specific web pages), they are automatically sent the next steps in the sequence by email, and so on and so forth to the point where your automation finishes, until the next trigger or a different automation sequence.

Can you imagine that? Well, it exists and it's available to you right now. This type of feature and more really take customer service and your delivery to the next level. Investing in a software service that has email automation, different automation triggers, tagging, segmentation and full reporting is what you're looking for. Why? This is where you find further leverage of your time. Can you imagine paying someone to do what was explained in the example above for every new client you enroll? Lots of time to do, not to mention human error would creep in. And, even if you're thinking this is too systemised, remember you're in control of the automation and you can simply inject break points where triggers require one of your team members to reply personally with a call or email so that human element remains. If you're not using this type of automation yet, now is the time.

Example automation sequences you can implement;

- **Welcome / On boarding** – Welcoming new clients with welcome packs, pdfs, links to videos, etc.
- **Programme Drip** – Scheduled emails that guide your customers through your programmes or products, week by week or day by day, etc.
- **Customer Upsell / Upgrade** – Introduce them to a new product or service.
- **Marketing Campaign Sequences** – Pre-scripted marketing messaged designed to convert more prospects into clients on autopilot through your marketing funnels.
- **Lead Cycler** – Run any leads who have been in your funnels but not purchased through an offer sequence until they come out the other end either buying or not.
- **Data Cleanse** – Run through any dead leads or prospects who have either not opened emails in 6/12 months and remove them from your lists.
- **Reactivation** – Any past customers who have not purchased in a set period of time (6 months) send out a reactivation sequence to get them buying again.

Customer Relationship Management

To be able to offer great customer service and support, you need to start from a place of servant delivery. Where your goal is to serve your clients, your team and yourself in the best way possible. And being able to know who your customers are, what services they have invested in with you, what products they have purchased from you and the different types of communication they've communicated with your team and any related partners to your company, is massively important in how your customers receive on-going value.

Managing customers, customer accounts (their records, purchase history, and profile) and taking care of how you communicate is very important. As you grow your business, your database is going to need a more sophisticated, yet simpler approach than simply referring and communicating with people based on past email communications and other ad-hoc options or tools.

Customer Relationship Management (CRM) Software is an important tool in your company's ability to grow and scale up in size.

How To Get Rid Of The Technology Headaches

For many coaches this is a big nemesis and pain. Fortunately for you and the many clients, I've helped, I turn this into something more manageable with fewer headaches. However, technology can and will go wrong when you need it to work at the best of times, but getting it close to perfect and working is all that you need.

If technology really isn't for you, find someone who can help you fix it. Outsource or employ someone to assist, otherwise, you'll waste precious time.

CHAPTER ACTION SUMMARY

- Know the difference in the 4 types of jobs and what you must work towards
- Create your outline for your own Client-Getting-System
  - Introduce automation to create even more time in your life and business
  - Use CRM software to remove the hassle of managing clients randomly

Refer to the MLMC Workbook to work on these key points.
www.moreleadsmoreclientsbook.com/resources

WHAT GETS MEASURED GETS IMPROVED
RETURN ON INVESTMENT
RECENCY, FREQUENCY, UNIT OF SALE
THE 5 WAYS FORMULA TO PROFIT
PROFIT
WHAT'S THE MOST EFFECTIVE METHOD?
TEST
WHY YOU'VE GOT TO PAY-TO-PLAY
GOOGLE
FACEBOOK
EMAIL MARKETING REGULAR & DAILY
MARKETING FUNNEL AUTOMATION EBM STYLE
DAILY / REGULAR EMAILS REGULAR EBM WITH PERSONALITY
NEWSLETTER / DIGEST EMAILS MORE FORMAL UPDATES WEEKLY / MONTHLY ETC
PERSONAL EMAILS ONE-TO-ONE
NEW ANNOUNCEMENT NEW OFFER OR SOMETHING HAPPENING
EVENT INVITES
SOCIAL MEDIA HYPE OR REAL?
HOW OFTEN YOU SHOULD BE MARKETING
MARKETING
MARKETING

Chapter 6

How To Get More Leads (The Tactics)

By now, you should understand what needs to be created (Strategy, positioning, direct marketing/offers, products/ services, and the systems/funnels you can use for leverage) and you're on your way to the next level. It's time to focus on the actual marketing tactics (the *promotion* of your product/service)and getting your message in front of your target audience. This is when you test your "Message to Market Match On The Right Media."

Marketing, According to Britannica…

"Marketing, the sum of activities involved in directing the flow of goods and services from producers to consumers."

What Gets Measured Gets Improved

To test how successful a campaign is, it comes down to what is measured. Even in its basic form, how many leads and prospects that convert to sales gives you a measurement. Many coaches and business owners focus on the wrong things. They say things like:

- I'm focused on my marketing funnel (building the web pages of their online marketing system).

- I created an amazing blog article (with zero social media following or comments, no engagement, never marketed).
- I created lots of videos and put them on my website (nobody or your target audience of a significant number know you yet).
- I'm creating the perfect images for my advertising campaigns.
- I've purchased a full page newspaper ad which will get me more clients.

You should create content but once they're complete, narrow the focus and begin promoting. Get it out and in the hands, eyes, and ears of your audience fast.

ROI – Return On Investment

Your Return On Investment (ROI) in marketing will result in a return to you, by way of leads, sales or some other targeted compensation or benefit. It's a principle that you target as a way of justifying the time and energy you put into a campaign, which is ultimately the reward for your efforts.

Recently, ROI has become a buzz-word and people will have conversations with agencies, their team or consultants, asking what's the ROI of this or that. When in actuality, they don't know what their target "return" should be.

For example: What's the ROI of building a relationship with a strategic partner that is going to introduce your products or services to their audience of 10,000 customers over the next 12 months, who are the very people you wish to attract? Or, what's the return on investment of continually putting out a weekly podcast of great content to your audience without seeing any immediate return?

With this in mind, I would suggest you focus on the ROI metrics that you wish to measure.

- Monetary
- Leads/customers
- Benefits to your business etc

Now, you can focus on how your marketing campaigns will get you the results you're going for. By understanding ROI from this context, for every pound or dollar invested in your marketing, how much is returned back to you - £1 in £2 out. You can only get to this value by first knowing your numbers.

Note: If math is not your favourite part of your business, I have an announcement for you. Deal with it. You're in business, and you need to know how the numbers work. This is not Einstein levels of math, just the basics of what your marketing campaigns need to be based on. Ignore the numbers, abdicate responsibility, and you'll end up broke.

Let's get into these numbers so you will have an understanding of what they mean.

Recency, Frequency, Unit of Sale

I learnt the following metrics (RFU) from the late great Direct Response Marketer, Gary C Halbert. RFU allows you to know how effective a list is (yours or an external database of leads/customers).

Recency – How recent your customers or an external list of leads have been marketed to.

Frequency – How often your customers or an external list have purchased from you or a partner in a given period of time.

Unit of Sale – The price of your products and services.

These three indicators (RFU) are what you or your team member need to keep track of. Remember, what gets measured gets improved.

The 5 Ways Formula To Profit

Now that you understand RFU, we need to bring the metrics together to know the profitability of your marketing campaigns and business in a more detail, so you know where to pin-point improvements and monitor results. I learnt the 5 ways formula from Brad Sugars.

The 5 Ways Formula

Leads × **Conversion Rate** = Customers

Customers × **Average Sale** × **Transactions** = Turnover

Turnover × **Margin (Costs)** = Profit

So the five variables highlighted are what you can affect. The others are a result of those five variables. You can use this formula to calculate the profitability of all your marketing tactics, including how profitable are your pay per click ads, social media organic posting, marketing campaign as a whole, email marketing and so on…

- Leads – The number of people you attract into your campaign.
- Conversion Rate – The rate at which you convert leads to customers.
- Average Sale – The Average value that you sell your products or services. E.g. (Total sales in a given period divided by the number of customers you sold to.)
- Transactions – How many times you sold to a customer in a given period.
- Margin – Your business overhead (costs) as an actual value for the period you choose

*Period/time – when calculating your results using the formula, choose a set period – a day, week or month, quarter or year, etc. Never mix up the period in the five areas when calculating. Simply perform one calculation for a week, then another for a month, etc.

Remember, turnover is for vanity, profit is for sanity. So stay sane with the five ways formula people.

What's the most effective method?

It's often the main question for the inquisitive coach or one that hasn't really done much marketing with enough info on the main channels available. The simple answer is... The ones that get you the results are the most effective. It's your job to Test, Test, and Test – and let the results show you. What works in one industry may not work in the next, which is why it's key to test FIRST.

Why You've Got To Pay-To-Play

The most prolific tools made available to attain vast and deep reach are a few clicks away. For the first time in the history of marketing, Facebook Ads and Google Ads have connected billions of people together, ready to be marketed to like never before. The playing fields have been levelled, the landscape of markets have been placed within reach of budgets, and small business owners can compete in their own niche with the "A Players" (the big companies) in the market. The costs are manageable and very competitive with huge return and reward possible.

I've achieved success with both Facebook Ads and Google Ads, but there is a disclaimer. These platforms can end up costing you a lot of money if done wrong. Coupled with the fact that as they've become more popular, the prices have risen as more people flood the platforms to get in front of their target audience. The proverbial golden-age has gone for both of these platforms, but they still remain gold mines in terms of tapping into your potential clients.

The key with both of these platforms is being aware of your numbers, your weekly and monthly marketing budget, your cost per lead and cost per client acquired. Often these numbers will reveal themselves as you begin to advertise and see the returns your advertising campaigns generate. I've found that as long as your advertising cost is outweighed by the front-end and back-end (sales and cash-flow), you achieve with your clients, your profitability from higher value products will make a big difference. If your prices and margins are low, it doesn't take a genius to realise you may end-up making a loss.

Let's explore both of these key platforms and you'll see the distinctions on how to use them.

Facebook Ads – Generally you're targeting people (on Facebook, Instagram, and The Audience Network) who are using these social media platforms as entertainment sources to watch videos, follow leaders, superstars and other popular brands as part of their individual interests. They can keep in touch with family and friends. Generally, it's not a place where people are actively searching for stuff, they are there to be entertained. So when your ads appear in front of these people, it must entertain and then educate (Edutainment). It must cause a "Pattern Interrupt."

Google Ads – When targeting people on Google Search and YouTube, understand these are two distinct channels. Google is a place where people are actively searching for information, either for research or to take the next steps in having a solution to their problem or need. YouTube is also a place where this type of usage takes place, but it also doubles up as an entertainment source. So your ad campaigns must take into consideration the mentality of the audience on both platforms and then deliver ads that fit the "search or entertainment" need.

I could go into the uses and exact methods of both platforms, but because of how regularly they are updated, it would be out of date by the time this book is released. If you'd like to find out more about the current best practices with these platforms, visit the following link for more information **www.moreleadsmoreclientsbook.com/resources**

Email Marketing- Regular and Daily

Email marketing is a confusing marketing tactic because it comes in many different guises. People still ask if it's effective with the amounts of emails the average person receives in their inbox? Do people even open the emails and who would want to receive a weekly or daily email? *The answer is yes*. The people you identified in your market research have a pain or a need, and they want more of what you have to offer to fulfil that desire. Email is the art of 1-to-1 communication in an age of mass noise; it can be used for:

- Marketing funnel automation – EBM style with SOS
- Daily/regular emails – Regular EBM with personality
- Newsletter/digest emails – More scheduled updates, weekly / monthly, etc
- Personal emails – 1-to-1 reaching out to specific people
- New Announcement – New offer or something happening
- Event invites– Invite people to your webinar, live stream or in person event

Social Media, Hype Or Real?

When it comes to Market, Message and the MEDIUM, social media is a key vehicle in delivering your message because of the massive number of people participating number into the hundreds of millions and billions, and the insights, statistics and data that you can tap into for your own advantage is huge!

Coaches are encouraged to get onto social media, start a Facebook Page, create Instagram and LinkedIn profiles and jump on Twitter. Coaches take the advice and action, expecting the masses of people to come running with a fist full of cash ready to hand over. But eventually, reality sets in... Tumbleweeds roll past, and the sound of crickets reverberates.

Coaches ask, "Where are they? Where are the customers they told me about?"

Like any marketing channel, you need to know what works and be ready strategically to roll out the tactics to capture the attention of your customers. You need to learn the rules of the game and remember your message to potential customers. Consistency, adapting to the market and channel are key. But this is so often missed.

For example. A coach joins Facebook and post a text update at the beginning of the week to their profile. They start looking at posts from other people and dig into the comments, while wasting time scrolling through other peoples updates, looking at friends or associates (not potential customers). Then, during the middle of the week, they post a picture or quote on their profile and a few people like it. Keep in mind, the average person on Facebook has 200-500 friends (a mix of actual friends, family, and people met at networking events – not prospective customers).

The week is over and the coach says, "Social media doesn't work."

It's at this point the question of there must be a better way to do this sets in. They then have a great idea… I know I will hire that person from the networking meeting to do my social media marketing and it will work because they know what to do… (Hmm, I wonder if the Coach has even considered the message and right place of finding their clients on Facebook?)

So the social media person is hired, they recommend writing some articles on your expertise, they will use this content to come up with ideas of messages to share. They do a month of posting for this coach. The results are a little better but no real leads have been generated. The social media consultant explains this is what happens and that over time it will work. After 3 months of social media posting, one sale was achieved for a low value and there has been some improvement, but nothing significant.

The Coach labels this as a failure… I've been there, it's an energy drain, and it's disheartening.

But throughout all of this, the basics were not actioned from the start "learn the rules of the game and remember your message to market match".

I don't know what it is, but I often see Coaches who learn the key step of focusing on their client's problems and related benefits, only to then put out messages and updates, pictures and videos that don't actually focus on the target audiences problems or needs. The message seems to be lost because of some advice here or someones opinion there and goes back to general (vanilla) stuff and misguided noise in the market. But, what I know that absolutely works is consistency of the basics using the EBM approach and direct response for your offers.

Side Note: Don't get caught up in the "likes game". This is a proven concept of human neuroscience whereas a population we're becoming reprogrammed thanks to the big social media platforms. We get a dopamine hit (a rush of happiness – similar to how a hug makes you feel) each time we receive likes, shares and comments on our social media content. It's been researched, by San Francisco-based media-buying firm RadiumOne, and it's pretty clear it's changing the fabric of how we interact as humans. So what I will say here without going too deep into this subject – is focus on the numbers that generate leads and sales. Don't read too much into the other things (E.g., not receiving many likes, views, comments or shares etc) unless they lead you to growth in your business.

A key step with social media is to understand how each platform works, then use direct response and storytelling to maximise your success... It's pretty simple if you are stuck, go to YouTube, search for "How to use [Your chosen social media platform - Website]" and you will find a plethora of videos explaining the basics and what you need to get going. To maintain marketplace presence will be down to you improving your craft, the delivery of your message, how you appear, the quality of your images and your videos. So with this in mind let's take a look at the current top platforms I use to get my message out to my audience.

Facebook

Facebook is not only the biggest platform for advertising online, in terms of reach, it's also a great place for you to create an audience – both B-2-B and B-2-C, whether that be on your personal profile, groups or your business page. It allows you to publish content in many different formats and gives you the tools for your message to reach your market. Like any platform, for example; Google, over time things get a little stricter, and there are more hoops to jump through as Facebook tightens up its features and policies, so it serves its audience better to offer a more authentic experience.

For me, Facebook started out as a networking site and soon became a go to place, for attracting in sales leads. I've created great connections and relationships as well as gaining new customers. Many of which have gone from being £2000 clients, then ascending them to higher back-end offers of £7500 and £15,000+. Not too shabby...

LinkedIn

LinkedIn Is generally known as a more professional social networking platform, where you tend to find more B-2-B related contacts and opportunities. Similar to Facebook you can post messages in many different formats and acts as a great vehicle to deliver your message via your personal profile, business page, groups and instant articles (LinkedIn's own inbuilt blog system).

I've created a number of opportunities on LinkedIn from Sales, JV partners to Podcast Guest Interviews (which help with positioning). One path to a sale came as a result of posting a message in a number of groups that linked to an Instant Article I created, this in-turn linked to an opt-in page in one of my marketing funnels. The key to the success of this example came from my follow-up. Another example was posting curiosity appealing post on my personal profile which resulted in attracting a JV partner who had a 2 million plus B-2-B database. This coupled with some offline calls sealed the opportunity. The vehicle was LinkedIn but the principles of direct response and prospect follow-up was essential in both examples.

Make sure to download my LinkedIn Guide which takes you through the key steps to attracting leads on LinkedIn and how I generated over £100k in 2 months using an organic marketing tactic.

www.moreleadsmoreclientsbook.com/resources

Instagram

Whilst many who know this platform think of it as a photo and short video clip channel, there are a number of features to be aware of. 1 – its owned by Facebook, which means you can reach more clients through paid advertising 2 – It has a big active daily user base 3 – There's a mix of B2B and B2C opportunities that can be explored simply by putting out the right message. One example I've used is to post longer article-style posts within the description of my pictures and using comments to add the longer (additional) pieces of content to my post; this has allowed me to fully target my audience resulting in leads and prospects in my marketing funnels. Direct links to pages are not possible although with some creative thinking, an excellent crafted sequence of messages and good old direct response outreach in messages, you can convert cold leads into clients, to the tune of thousands.

YouTube

Video is the main medium for marketing online, and the main place for video is YouTube. It holds many opportunities and has seen the rise in recent years of the "Millionaire YouTuber". Basically people who make money from creating popular and engaging videos in specific niches, where they receive money from sponsors, endorsement deals and through Google's (AdSense) System, which pays them for all the views they receive.

I've experienced my own success from doing a business marketing show over a 6 month period, where we provided content to help people market their businesses better, this lead to leads and actual clients. As people watched the content, trust was established by using the EBM formula and this lead to many £5000 - £20,000 opportunities. The key was consistency and simply showing up when we said we would for our weekly shows. If you're thinking about YouTube, look at creating both free organic video content and paid advertising through the Google Ads Platform.

Twitter

Twitter, one of the original big social media platforms holds an opportunity if you can invest the time required, which is true of any channel. Through followers and our audience on Twitter, this helped to gain support for our podcast in terms of votes when we needed their help for voting us to win "The Best Business Podcast" award in 2015. Engagement in more recent years hasn't been as high, and I believe this is because of the saturation of the platform. But I would advise anyone to test it for 3 months as a minimum to see what results it can generate for your business in terms of leads and sales. In terms of the social media platforms I've listed above, Twitter has been the least in priority for me, but I recommend you test for yourself and see what level of lead generation or marketing exposure it can help you gain.

How often you should be marketing...

One of the big failures of many Coaches is how much time they actually invest in marketing their business. Most seem to get caught up in either creating a new website, creating a new guide, perfecting their logo, focusing on one tactic like SEO or Social Media, but have very little or no focus on actual lead generation.

This may seem strange but it's a disease, it's an epidemic – and too many coaches who are struggling can't seem to shift it, but I need to raise this point to the top and answer it for you right now.

The reality is that without new clients or new sales, you're in a dying business, trust me I've been there, and the reality is that the coaches who are succeeding at marketing recognize this. It's too easy to abdicate the responsibility of marketing your business, because even if you have a team member, outsource partner or you work with an agency who provides you with marketing services, you have to keep your eye on the ball. Even if marketing isn't your strongest skill, from a strategic point of view, you've got to know the rules of the game – no ifs no buts!

Actual working time on marketing and lead generation should be at least 2 hours a day if you're the only person in your business if you have a team it should be a full time role at minimum. And when should you stop marketing? When things are going great or when you have a holiday?

Continual Never Ending Marketing is the reality of your business, just like the operations and serving your clients never stops (so long as you have clients). The time that you decide to stop marketing and focusing on lead generation is when you decide to close your business.

CHAPTER ACTION SUMMARY

What you need to put into Action

- Understand what needs to be measured in your marketing results
- Work out the ROI you plan to achieve and compare to the reality of your results. Re-adjust and go again.
- Monitor your RFU
- Track results and use the 5 ways formula. Keep on testing, find out what works
- Use paid advertising to grow your reach
- Use email marketing to create deeper communication with your prospects and clients
- Use social media to get results
- Keep marketing, always!

Refer to the MLMC Workbook to work on these key points.

www.moreleadsmoreclientsbook.com/resources

In the workbook add the 90-day timetable and marketing tactics to do.

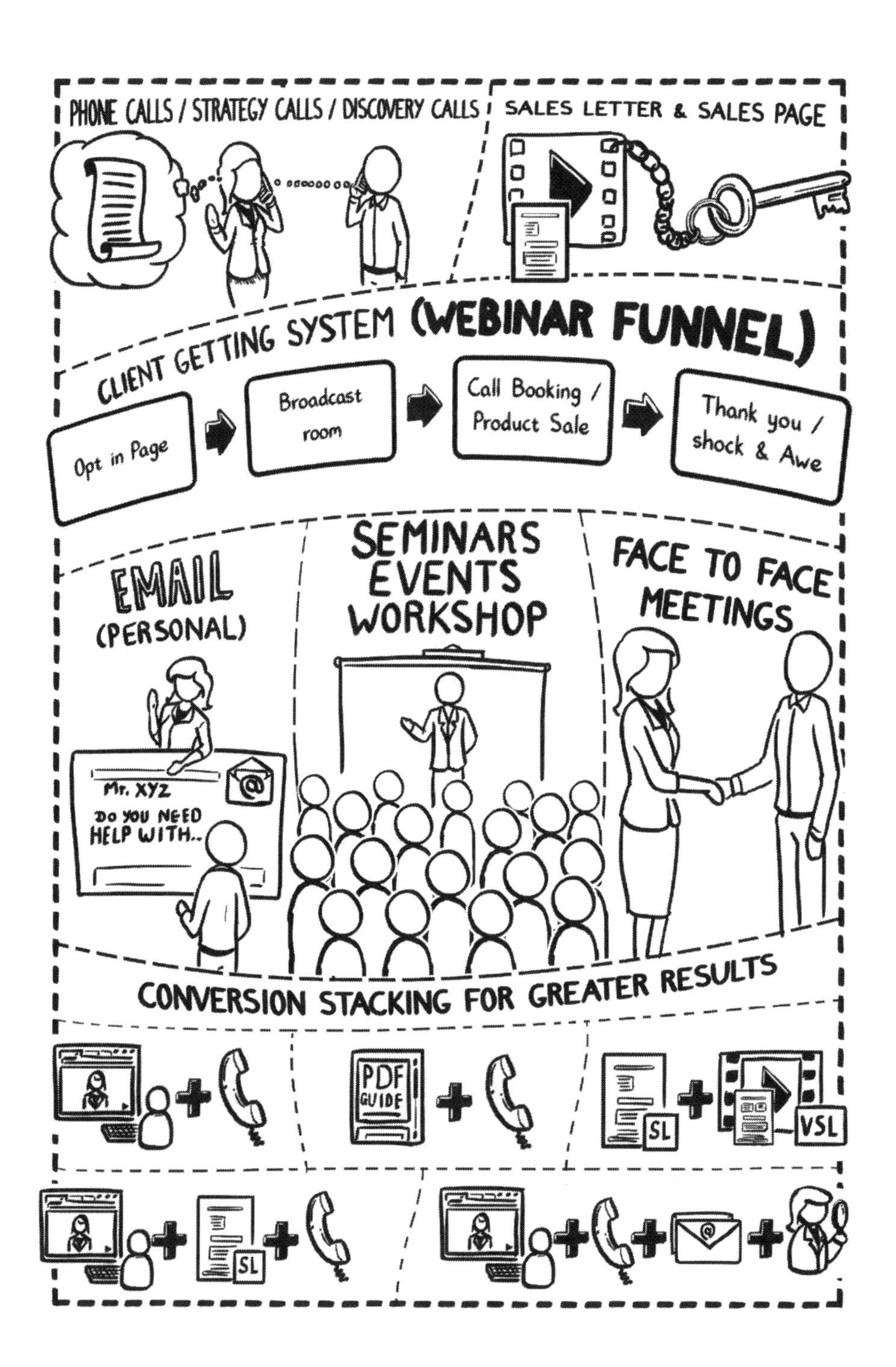
PHONE CALLS / STRATEGY CALLS / DISCOVERY CALLS
SALES LETTER & SALES PAGE
CLIENT GETTING SYSTEM (WEBINAR FUNNEL)
Opt in Page
Broadcast room
Call Booking / Product Sale
Thank you / shock & Awe
EMAIL (PERSONAL)
Mr. XYZ
DO YOU NEED HELP WITH..
SEMINARS EVENTS WORKSHOP
FACE TO FACE MEETINGS
CONVERSION STACKING FOR GREATER RESULTS
PDF GUIDE
SL
VSL
SL

CHAPTER 7

How to Convert More Prospects into Clients

Converting prospects into paying clients is the goal of the sales function in your business. A business without paying clients is no business at all, so with this in mind, you need solid methods that will result in converting prospects. Fortunately, there are a number of great conversion methods. All differ in subtle ways and will have a positive impact in your sales performance when done right.

Phone Calls / Strategy Calls / Discovery Calls

For me, sales calls, discovery calls or strategy calls are powerful conversion methods when it comes to selling High Value Services. The better prepared you are, the more they lead to a sale. When stacked with another conversion method like webinars, the calls become powerful because the prospect comes to you qualified, having been indoctrinated with your training. Then, choosing to invest 30 – 60 minutes of time with you to help fix their problem.

Hearing another human being on the phone or even seeing them on a video call allows you to display empathy and take a person from their old ways to new concepts and methodologies that you have created to help them move closer toward their goals. This first stage transformation is key to converting a prospect into a client, and it's a great way to start your Coach and Client relationship.

The good thing about these types of calls is that they can be prepared for in advance and whether or not you're new to sales calls, the skills can be learnt pretty quickly. For best results, use a script (we offer our clients the Secret Sales Script). If you're worried, people won't know you're reading from a script and THEY ARE a good thing.

Let me break it down quickly. Ever been to a movie at the cinema or a theatre performance, where you've really enjoyed it and bought into the idea of the story and the characters? Maybe you had a tear in your eye or your partners when you watched something really emotional… Well, these emotions were created off the back of a movie actor or actress fulfilling their role in the movie or show having read a script!

Even the greats of Hollywood believe in them. The key is to do the work and practice. Role play and build up your confidence and skills around this fundamental key to your business. In time, you will truly understand how to flow and direct a conversation. You'll know when to listen and when to speak, when to take back control if a prospect goes off on a tangent and how to keep them in the state of wanting to change, how to test if they're really committed, how to use their own past experiences to bring about a decision for change and how to manage and handle objection. These give you more room to continue a conversation where you're still in control that will ultimately allow you to determine whether this person is right for your service or product and whether your product is right for the prospect so that you sell from a place of integrity.

In the next chapter "How to sell more" I deep dive into the noble art of selling with scripts and more…

Sales Letter & Sales Page

The Sales Letter was covered early on in this book, due to the size of impact that a good sales letter will have on any business…

Video Sales Letter (VSL)

The Video Sales Letter is an extension of the sales letter, in video format. The video allows you to hit home more on the human senses. A good point to mention is that they don't require extensive setup and are actually very straightforward to create, in its simplest format you create a narrated text only PowerPoint video (recorded on a computer). And with this low barrier to creating a VSL, they can be iterated very quickly as you tweak and improve what the VSL contains to maximise conversions.

To find out more about VSL's check out my interview with Jon Benson, the guy who created the first "ugly" Video Sales Letter (the VSL) in 2007. Access the Jon Benson Interview here - Visit www.moreleadsmoreclientsbook.com/resources

Webinar

Although we've discussed webinars earlier in the book, there are a few steps to consider, try performing a number of live webinars and or possibly recording a few test runs to help perfect your delivery of the content, be comfortable with the technical aspects of hosting a webinar and then actually creating a webinar that not only generates you registrations (leads) but also prospects (applications for your services or products) plus sales where you're selling directly from a webinar.

Email (Personal)

Personal emails are a very good conversion method too, as they are a follow on from your prior activity. When you've built trust and established a relationship, and a prospect has invested time (your EBM content) and possibly some money (purchasing a trip wire or attending your event), now the prospect has become more indoctrinated into your message and what you can offer them. Follow through by checking on your CRM and the data that you have on the prospects, or even communications you may have had on phone, email or possible instant messenger. You can then close the sale by sending out a tailored email notifying them of a new product/service, asking them to commit as they've been interested previously, but not acted on up until now or simply to present a new idea that you will help them with.

Email example:

Subject: Hey OR [FIRST NAME]

[FIRST NAME],

Do you still need help with [problem - marketing]?

Leon Streete

Seminars / Events / Workshops

Another effective method to convert prospects into clients are events. They open the doors to many opportunities and are great when it comes to closing deals and most importantly cash injections. There are many different types of events you can run, from seminars with 100+ people to events under 100 people. More intimate workshop style events with the numbers from 5 to 30 people. They all work in different ways, yet can be used to successfully convert prospects to clients.

The key is to understand the goal of your event. Why are you holding it? To build your brand, generate leads, increase trust and put yourself in a position of targeting sales of your products or services? Your event must be designed to strategically sell your products or services. It must be planned out and crafted to deliver value, present some form of actionable content, answer all potential objections a prospect would have before becoming a your client and finally close the deal and make sales.

So, what can you expect from events as a result to even consider it? A friend of mine from Texas, Markus Heitkoetter – investor coach, devised a strategy that allowed him to convert $290k worth of programme sales from workshops of 60-80 people in one month period. I witnessed J.T Foxx (top speaker/coach) close £500k worth of business after a 90 minute talk. Both phenomenal results. With this in mind, I'm sure you'd agree events are worth considering as one of your conversion methods.

Events cost money to put on, but they do not have to cost a lot. You can budget to ensure you have your costs to a minimum, whilst providing a great customer experience. You may decide to hold a free event where you subsidise the event cost with your products or service sales. It can also be paid in advance where the ticket money can be used to pay for the venue, audiovisual and any catering needed. The difference with a paid event is that you have someone who is willing to invest money compared to someone who is there for a free event. It's important, because that means you already have a buyer.

Download the extra bonus 14 steps of running your own event here: **www.moreleadsmoreclientsbook.com/resources**

Face to Face Meetings

Following closely behind sales calls and events in terms of closing ratio results, face to face meetings are a good place to be dropped into the deep end. This is truly being in the trenches, understanding how you respond and managing your emotions. It's where you learn about human psychology and what it takes to influence and persuade someone to buy your product or service.

These sales situations help you to build your character and skills fast, because you learn to use the power of asking questions to first qualify and diagnose, then present your offer and close the sale. Role playing and preparation for your meeting is paramount. During your meeting, take notes and refer to them during your meeting. It demonstrates good listening and attention.

Always call your prospect 24 hours, then 2 hours before your meeting to ensure all is ok and that they are still able to meet up. It shows how committed to the meeting you are and it gets them to commit to you. There's nothing more annoying than traveling to a meeting, only to find out they forgot or they double booked, and you're the meeting they dropped.

Go with the intention of being able to help the person you're about to meet, knowing that the only way they'll get that help is if they invest in your product or service. Sell with integrity. If they are not a good fit, then walk away or recommend a strategic partner who could help them further.

Conversion Stacking For Greater Results

When you combine your conversion methods, you can truly end up with winning sales figures. The key is that each technique adds more trust, intimacy and allows you to close more clients.

Example combinations…

- Webinar + Phone Call
- PDF Guide + Phone Call
- Sales Page + VSL
- Webinar + Sales Page + Call
- Webinar + Call + Email + Personal Follow-ups

After testing, choose the methods that get results and best suits you.

CHAPTER ACTION SUMMARY

What you need to put into Action

- Close higher value deals using Phone Calls / Strategy Calls / Discovery Calls
- Leverage your marketing with a Sales Letter & Sales Page
- Add multimedia using Video Sales Letter (VSL) and Webinars
- Use personal emails, to connect and re-engage
- Host Seminars / Events / Workshops for added sales opportunities
- Stack conversion options For Greater Results...

Refer to the MLMC Workbook to work on these key points.

www.moreleadsmoreclientsbook.com/resources

SELLING
THE JOB AND SKILL OF PERSUADING PEOPLE TO BUY THINGS
QUALIFYING THE RIGHT PROSPECTS
NEED
USE
WANT
AFFORD
HOW TO CLOSE HIGH VALUE OFFERS
PRE-CALL
DURING THE CALL
WRAP UP CALL PHASE
OBJECTIONS
?#!$%
WHAT TO DO WHEN YOUR PROSPECT SAYS
NO!
THE ART OF FOLLOWING UP
BAMFAM
@
SMS
KNOWING THE MAIN OBJECTIONS
IT COSTS TOO MUCH
IT WON'T WORK FOR ME
I NEED TO SPEAK TO MY PARTNER
NEED TIME TO THINK IT THROUGH
I INVESTED IN THE PAST AND IT DIDN'T WORK OUT
I WASN'T PREPARED TO BUY TODAY
I'M JUST NOT READY TO MAKE A DECISION YET

Chapter 8

How To Sell More Products & Services

Where ever you are on this journey, selling is about practice, preparation and then using this skill as much as possible to get better. There's a saying from a top sales trainer I interviewed that cuts straight to the point of being honest with yourself so that you act daily when it comes to selling.

> "If you're not selling every day, then you're rusty"
>
> Grant Cardone.

Unless you're selling every day, you're not maxing out this skill or the ability to achieve the results that this vital function offers your business.

Let's look at the definition of selling according to Cambridge Dictionary;

> *"the job and skill of persuading people to buy things"*

I also understand that some people will have a negative idea of what it means to sell, this may be from a bad experience, stories from friends, family or the news. That has now skewed their perspective of what it means to sell or be a salesperson.

Like most things, your perspective will be down to your mindset, and when it comes to selling, mind-set is the foundation that sales success is built on. It will include; your character, attitude, fears, insecurities and confidence. And when you're speaking to a prospective high value clients, this will be evident, to them in how they hear you talk, your tone, how they see your body language and facial expressions and finally in the energy that you exude, which all combine to give them a feeling of confidence in listening to you.

Qualifying The Right Prospects

Qualifying is the ability to determine if the person you are speaking to or communicating with has the authority and the means to make a buying decision. This part of the sales process is a big time-saver when you do it right.

Four Questions Every Top Coach Must Answer For Qualifying

To qualify effectively, you need to know who you are dealing with. That can only be done by gathering data. Top sales trainer and expert Brian Tracey recommends four questions.

1. **Does the prospect need what you're selling?** It may seem obvious, but selling with integrity is all about presenting something you know will help the prospect.
2. **Can the prospect use what you're selling?** Many people may want something but can it be used or integrated into to their life or business?
3. **Can the person afford what you're selling?** Do they have the budget or means to invest in what you have to offer?
4. **Does the person want the product?** Through effective communication and listening skills, you are now four steps closer to closing the sale.

Surveys and Questionnaires

To maximise your marketing and sales, consider using surveys and questionnaires to gain feedback. You gain valuable insight into who your prospects are and set yourself up right to deal with the best potential clients. The cool thing about setting up surveys is that they can be systemised into your marketing funnels and are a great way to setup and continue to benefit from the responses they gather.

Example "Business-To-Business" questions you can use in your surveys, application forms or on a short call include;

- What is your number one challenge right now when it comes to (*Insert here: What you help your clients solve.* E.g. Online Marketing, Growing Your Business, Your Career, Mindset)?
- What does your ideal business/life look like?
- What do you do for your clients and what are you currently charging?
- Over the past two years how much have you invested in training, personal development or coaching? (This is good to know if they already buy in the area of coaching)
- What is your level of commitment to start, out of 10? (This tells you if they're serious about making change)
- Then the obvious, name, email and phone number.

How To Close High Value Offers

There are 3 key stages when it comes to selling high value products or services that I use and these stages work time and time again to ensure you get the results.

1. Pre-call
2. During The Call
3. Wrap Up Call Phase

1 – Pre-call

The pre-call is all about having your marketing do its job. Earlier I mentioned that the marketing stage is responsible for 80% of the pre-sell. And as part of that pre-sell, a prospect will have been taken through your marketing funnel to a stage where they will be offered an opportunity to find out more about the coaching service or programme you offer. This may be done as an application form, survey or questionnaire. It can also be a short phone call after receiving a response from an opt-in form (name, email and phone number) which was submitted in exchange for some of your valuable EBM content.

Generally, anything over £2000 has to be sold either over the phone or in person, depending on your relationship with the prospect or the nature of your industry.

2 – During The Call

With the prospect's details submitted, you're now in a position to make the call with enough information to help you determine how you structure the first 10 minutes. Get into a state of mind that is heightened ready for both of you to experience a "Win, Win". First, you need to establish rapport and set the agenda of the call. You are here to listen to them, not coach.

The Questions:

- To start with, what is it that made you decide to invest the time today to grow your business/improve your life etc?
- Fantastic– tell me more about you/your business/your current situation?
- Imagine if you and I were working together, I teach you everything I know and how to get the results you desire, and you could wave a magic wand and have everything exactly the

way you wanted it within a year, what would your business/life/ health look like?

- Now what do you think could possibly be currently stopping you from getting to those goals?
  - o How long has this been a challenge for you?
- What have you tried so far and what resources, connections, talents or skills can you use to make this happen?
- Where do you need my help in achieving your goals?

Why these types of questions? It's simple, fact-finding and emotion. "Logic Makes People Think – Emotion Makes People Act".

3 – Wrap Up Call Phase

The wrap-up call phase is all about presenting your offer, service or programme. Usually, this is referred to in many sales scenarios as "the close." You're now moving into the place of assured confidence and integrity. With the information the prospect shared with you about their goals, problems, and resources, you must be clear that you can help them.

Ask...

1. "Let me ask you this... Where are you on a scale of 1 to 10... 1 being you're not committed to 10 being I'm absolutely committed would you say you're at right now?"
   - This question is paramount as it will get your prospects certainty levels to the highest before you ask for the order. If they say anything less than 10 you must let them know that between 2-9 does not exist, and you have to be 10 out of 10 committed for change to take place!
2. So I only have one more question. Do you want me to help you?
   - Wait... If they answer "yes," now ask.

3. I have a program designed specifically to help people overcome these type of challenges – shall I tell you about it?
    - Wait… If they answer "yes," now ask.
4. Describe your programme and continually tie back to how it meets their goals and helps them overcome their challenges.
    - Ask: Does that sound like the type of thing you are looking for?
    - Explain the fees and ask, "Would you prefer to make the full payment and or do monthly instalments work best for you?"

Objections

It's at this point you may get your first objection. This is where the sale really starts, so prepare to loop and go back into a second presentation. Remember you've qualified the prospect and allowed them to get this far with you. If you don't close nobody wins. Not you or them. Prepare to handle the objection by using these three steps, Agree. Address. Advance.

The only reason they haven't agreed to proceed is because the value of the money they have is worth more than the outcome you are presenting. If you "loopback" then you get another opportunity to build value on your offer. Just follow the four-step close and explore each step further. Be willing to loop up to 3-5 times!

What To Do When Your Prospect Says "No!"

In many cases, this is one of the most daunting aspects of selling for those low in confidence or fearful of a person saying no – even very confident sales people. The reality is that an objection in a selling situation is actually an opportunity to answer a question and turn that answer into a sale. Objections come in many shapes and forms, and your job is to seek them out, answer them confidently and move the prospect to stage of making a decision to go ahead (or not) once all areas have been explored.

Objections come up as first responses to test the sales person and it's your job to find out if the objection is real and valid.

Objection Examples and How to Handle Them

A real objection is a valid, existing reason for not taking up the proposition. When it's overcome, the sale is made. An objection from a prospect is not the end of the sales opportunity; it's the opportunity to continue the conversation until all objections are answered. If they are still not ready to buy from you or you feel they are not right at this time, then the close will not happen.

Let's take a closer look at the three steps Agree, Address and Advance.

1. Agree with the prospect
2. Address their issue
3. Advance them through to closing

These are the seven types of objections that may arise and insight on how to handle them.

1. ***It Costs Too Much*** – Do they understand the difference between price and value? Did you present your USP and unique mechanism in a way that clearly sets you apart from the competition?

   Your Response: Hey I totally agree and I've been in the situation where I've seen the price and my head has totally exploded. The key is not how much my programme costs, but how much getting the solution to your problem is worth to you. There's no such thing as a solution to a problem that is too expensive. There's only those people who aren't willing to do what it takes to get the problem solved. I'm ready to do what it takes for you. Are you ready to do what it takes for yourself? Let's do this!"

2. ***It won't work for me*** – They are looking for validation that there will not be a way for them to get a result or change because in the past what they have committed to, whether in part or not at all, didn't work.

   Your Response: I totally hear that I really do. I think sometimes the knee jerk response is, "What if it doesn't work?" I've been there many times before where I've thought, "What if this doesn't work for me? What if I can't get the result?" What I've got to say is, what if this does work? What differences would your life have if this did happen for you? What if you had me alongside you where we could ensure that this would work? How does that sound to you? And, believe me when I say, if you even have half the results that most people get when they work with me, you'll be very, very impressed. Sound fair enough?
3. ***I need to speak to my partner about this*** – They aren't confident in their own decision making or need some type of approval from a partner.

   Your Response: What you're really saying is you want to do this, you need to make this happen, but you're worried that your partner might not support you. Is that correct? Fantastic, I want to reward you for saying that out loud. Has your partner always been a detractor of your business? I can understand, you've been telling me it's been a difficult time over the past (*few years, etc – however long they've had the problem*). All the evidence they have is that you're a loser that can't make it. That sucks...
   So I want to reassure you, going to them and asking for their permission to change this isn't going to change anything... Going to them and saying hey I've made this choice and I need to do this, that's going change everything. I want to remind you, you said these things are really important, you wanted to change this because of the difficulties you've experienced and the future you want to create. So there's two ways this can go. One – You

go to them and say,"Hey I am scared that I don't have enough money to do this course and I know I've been churning around and not making the money, not providing for you and I'm really scared I don't know if I should do it or not."

When you do that what will your partner say? "Ah that's cool, you should spend the money even though you haven't been pulling your weight and doing a bad job." They will say "If you're going to go about this in a wishy-washy way and you're not sure you should do it, well it sounds like it's going to be a complete waste of money."If you go to them half arsed, that's exactly how they will respond.

Or two – you go to them and say, "Hey I know I haven't been cutting it. I know I haven't been doing as well as I should have andI'm pissed off.I've drawn a line in the sand, and I'm doing something about it. I've gotten some help and I've found a person who can help me with it. But I need you to be with me on this. I need your emotional support. The next year is going to be a wild ride and we're going to bust out of this situation. And I'm gonna give you all of the things that I haven't been able to give you."

So if you go to them with that kind of certainty, and tell them what you're going to do and ask them for their support, do you reckon you'll get a different answer? Yes good. [*Contrast close*] Which one of those people are you going to be? Well in that case. Visa or MasterCard?

4. ***Need Time to Think It Through*** – They are expressing either something they have not revealed previously, they haven't checked with a partner, checked on their financial position it could be that they truly don't have the money or finance available. But if you judge it to be avoidance or an excuse you can simply express to them the power of action or staying where they are not actually doing anything and continuing to lose out to the

benefits (including money and time) of what your products or service offer.

Your Response: I agree. A lot of people have to go away and really consider their options, but one thing that I've learned is that thought is instant. Just like when I say, "Blue Orange." There's not a Blue Orange around, but you see a Blue Orange in your head right? The question I've got is, what did you see that made you want to think about it? Is there any part of what has been presented that you thought you're a bit unsure of? Maybe it's me, maybe it's the service, maybe something else? I'd love to find out more. You can spend a few extra minutes with me now, and get this over with, then instead of spending more time with me tomorrow. You can use that time to make up for the few extra minutes it takes to do this deal right now. Let's go. You ready?

5. ***I invested in the past, and it didn't work out*** – They are sceptical and are questioning their own ability to trust again

   Your Response: I'm totally with you. I've done that so many times, because I'm like you. I've got the desire to make things happen. Let's face it, there are a lot of people out there that do sell bogus programs, bogus products, and we've invested and we've been hit very, very hard. One thing I see with you is you have the desire and all you lack is the direction, and we wouldn't have got to this point if we didn't know that we could both help each other out one hundred percent along the way. This time I know it's going to be different. Believe me; if you even get half the results most of the people get with me, you'll be very, very impressed. Sound fair enough?

6. ***I wasn't prepared to buy today*** – They have not been exposed to enough of your EBM content, but have a problem and they're interested in your solution. It may simply mean that this process has moved quicker than what they're used to, that's ok.

Your Response: I agree with you on being prepared before you make a buying decision. No one wants to be sold on something before they need it. When we were talking earlier, you said this was exactly what you needed –is that right? I'm not sure how long you've been putting your needs off, but that's never a good thing. Whether you buy today or a year from now, you're going to end up buying. Why wait any longer than absolutely necessary to solve your problem and fill your needs? Let's get this over with and get you on-board the programme."

7. ***I'm just not ready to make a decision yet*** – They are undecided and possibly procrastination has crept into their decision-making process.

   Your Response: I agree 100% that making a decision takes preparation. That's what I'm here to do for you. Prepare you to make a decision. We both know you need the product. You like it. It solves your problem. The longer you go without making a decision, the longer you'll have this problem. Let me help you. Would you like to make one payment or the flexible monthly option?

The Art Of Following Up

You may read this and assume, yeah I know it's important. But how often people actually follow-up is actually alarming. For some strange reason, mostly down to human psychology and probably lack of a good CRM system to monitor and remind the person, it is missed out. Think about this, you've invested your time and money to build your business, create a marketing strategy, acted on the marketing plan, finally your campaigns have run generating you leads, then the actual follow-up process is missed. It makes no sense. But if we dig a little deeper, it will.

Whether it's following up on sales leads, prospects, aftercare (post sale), follow-on support and more – the point is to follow up. Not to the point where you have called and maybe left a message, but to the point where you've had real communication and the other person has confirmed that they have received your message and acted on the follow up with a decision whether it's a Yes or No.

You need an answer, so you close the loop in your prospect chain, you attracted them into your marketing funnel, and now it's time to on-board them or not. Don't let their lack of response deter you either. I've followed up on prospects in one case for 14 months and they eventually became a client. I've followed up on leads when it's been the twelfth communication in a matter of weeks, so I could get a No and simply take them out of my active prospect list to make space for fresh prospects. I've followed up where the client has said yes just because of how determined I was to get an answer rather than being lead down the path of no-where.

And to me, the art of following up is never about you and what they will think of you. It's all about getting an answer so you and the prospect can move on. Whether that's with them being a client or not right now.

To improve your follow-up process, book a meeting from a meeting (BAMFAM). So when you're either in the meeting or on a call, book in a follow-up date before you finish up. That way you're getting commitment from the prospect to make space for an answer at a future date. This has worked particularly well for me over the years, not just in sales situations but also in general client communication when I need to book in follow-up and forthcoming dates for communication.

CHAPTER ACTION SUMMARY

What you need to put into Action

- Qualify the right prospects using the Four Questions Every prospect Must Answer
- Use Surveys and Questionnaires to automate this as much as possible
- Close High Value Offers using
  - Pre-call
  - During The Call
  - Wrap Up Call Phase
- Remember when a prospect says no, it's not the end of the sale
- Handle objections confidently, practice the response out loud and role play.
- Follow-up at least 12 time, most people give up after the first time....

Refer to the MLMC Workbook to work on these key points.
www.moreleadsmoreclientsbook.com/resources

THE JOURNEY OF AN ENTREPRENEUR
WHAT PEOPLE THINK IT LOOKS LIKE
WHAT IT REALLY LOOKS LIKE
CASH FLOW TO A BUSINESS IS LIKE OXYGEN TO A HUMAN
CASH FLOW
THEY DID IT, NOW IT'S YOUR TURN
DOING IT ALONE IS A MYTH...
THE ACTOR AL PACINO IN "CARLITO'S WAY"
"WHEN YOU CAN'T SEE THE ANGLES NO MORE YOU'RE IN TROUBLE, BABY."
GET A COACH
LONG TERM PLANNING, SHORT TERM FOCUS.
(TEAM)
TOGETHER EVERYONE ACHIEVES MORE
T E A M
HOW TO CREATE YOUR VERY OWN TIME MACHINE

Chapter 9

How To Take Your Business To The Next Level

You've seen the picture before, the journey of an entrepreneur. What you think it will be like, compared to what it's actually like. There's up, down, left, right, back, forth and many times round in circles. Yes, the result of achieving your goal is paved with gold, or at least whatever it is you've set your sights on, but it takes grit, determination, and thick skin. You need to be able to take the hits, get knocked down and then get back up and dust yourself off. You will truly have to come out of your comfort zone because it's actually the place that holds you back and limits your success.

Entrepreneurship is more about your mental strength, attitudes and character than anything else. Whether you're motivated and positive more than anyone you know, running a business challenges you. It takes you beyond anything you've learnt and if you're an established coach, you know what I'm talking about. If you're new – welcome to the club. The rules are stay in the game no matter what!

To best prepare to tackle the worthy goal of growing your coaching business, look at the greatest businesses that exist and the local businesses you admire. What do they have in common? They both have similar traits, advisors and a team!

Advisors who guide them on the best practices, recommendations, general advice. They also act as a sounding board, offer accountability and a good kick-up-the-butt when needed. The team is where you truly buy back your time and freedom, so you're not a slave to the job. Don't let being a business owner or self-employed with staff fool you into thinking you're beyond a job, especially if you're working 50+ hour weeks doing £10 an hour tasks.

Let's explore the types of people you need, but before that what else is there beyond people, what else remains?

Cash flow To A Business Is Like Oxygen To A Human

No matter the size of your business, cash-flow is king or queen – simple. You could be turning over £1million, and you're outgoings are £1.1 million. Yes it's a little extreme but it happens. People can get easily obsessed with the wrong things like team member issues, marketing, accounts, and customer care, etc. But the reality is this; if there is no money in the bank, you're screwed. You'll face more challenges with less options available to tackle them.

If you're going to grow your business, make sure your eyes are on your cash flow. I'm not saying ignore your purpose, customers, and everything else, but where your attention goes, your energy flows. If your attention includes keeping track of your cash-flow, this too will benefit.

It's difficult to grow a business when your creative and innovative ideas are stifled by scarcity, worry, and stress around making ends meet. It's a challenging place and until you go through it no one can truly explain how you will react or take it. To limit any potential of this occurring with you, keep this important business indicator at the forefront of your mind as you pursue growing and scaling your company.

What's the upside of good cash-flow? Well...you give yourself room to think and space to breath. Your mind can be filled with innovation and creative solutions, rather than limiting thoughts around paying bills, salaries and other commitments for your business and home. Whether you're making hundreds of thousands or millions, do yourself a favour and make sure this has your daily and weekly attention.

They Did It; Now It's Your Turn

Presidents have advisors, celebrities have managers, actors have directors, and athletes have coaches. Doing it alone is a myth...

One of the fastest routes to results and breakthroughs, and knowing what to do instead of feeling hopeless without options is with coaching.

You don't know what you don't know!

It's hard to explain to others why I invested so heavily in coaching? It's difficult to explain until you've been coached, held accountable and really taken to the next level. Not because of the results it helps you to achieve, but also the transformation, which is different and unique for everyone.

Imagine for a moment...

You decide to learn a new skill to take you toward a vague goal that will take you three to four years to master. You go through late nights, early mornings, and sometimes you will have to depend on others to help you. They don't actually know the right way, but have an idea none the less. As time passes, you need to ensure you have money coming in to pay for food, clothes, shelter, and travel.

The place that you attend to attain this skill will end up costing you £30,000 - £50,000, which most of it will be paid through a loan that will follow you for years. You complete the training and you are not guaranteed any sales or income. This place is known as "University…"

What if you were propositioned with this scenario as a valid way to start your business? You have the certificate AND THE DEBT to show for it. In the business world, this would be unacceptable and a dead-end story. Yet, society accepts this as the norm and since the majority of people live this life, they are sold the lie. I went to university and graduated, but as I look back, I haven't used it for gain or to get me anywhere I needed to be in business for the past 10 years. The skills that I use from my time at university have been good, but was the price worth it..? Would it be considered a sound investment? No.

With this story, I reinforce the power of finding a coach or mentor who can help you attain the results you're seeking in your business or from yourself. The key to this being a success stems from what we discussed earlier in how you identified your market and niche. When you have a goal to achieve in your business, you'll discover your need or a problem. You will want to conclusively make this happen, so you do what will get you there in the best way possible and the fastest.

Find someone who's already done what you're aiming to do. Someone who has walked a similar path and got the result or did even better than your goal. This is the key to being coached. Just like what Al Pacino said (in his infamous New York accent) in *Carlito's Way*, "When you can't see the angles no more you're in trouble, baby."

Those angles are the things you don't know, the opportunities you miss, the nuances, and the awareness level. This is why you invest in a coach. They have been there, done that, and got the t-shirt. You invest in a coach who has attained the result in either the submarket that you're targeting or in using the strategy/tactics that you wish to use.

It's simple really, but quite often coache send up with the wrong coach because they don't know what they actually need. They can't see the angles and the coach they hired has sold them onto their services not being able to help in a way that the person really needs.

Through being coached, I've had many revelations, breakthroughs, experienced great results, transformation in my skills, my mind-set, smashing through limiting beliefs, and understanding who I am as opposed to what I've learnt in society that has not served me. For many people who do not run their own business or work in a company that uses coaching, they will not get it – period. That's ok. I mean damn, they don't even get why you run your own business and that's okay. It's your journey to live, not anyone else's.

After being coached for over 10 years, the usual approach I take is to find out where my client is (when it comes to their business and life). Like building a house, you need to know the foundation is good in order to lay the first brick. So with a client you have to see where they are, their challenges, and their goals and then you can analyse what will be needed to help move them from where they are to where they want to be.

As a coach, I'm essentially the bridge to my client's goals with marketing and growing their business. It's then my job to work with them to identify where the specific help is needed (entrepreneur, manager or technician level), whilst keeping them on track with the vision they have. It's a dynamic route that bends to the uniqueness of each client, whilst keeping the destination of where I am helping them to get to as their north star.

A final point to mention, as a coach, don't fool yourself into not having your own coach. You're in the business of growth and accountability, so whether you have one, two or three coaches for different things in your life, make it happen sooner rather than later.

Long-Term Planning, Short-term focus.

To have massive focus in business, one of the best ways I've found is to work in 90-day blocks. Many successful entrepreneurs and businesses use the 90-day period as a key way to get the results they desire and you can split them down into 3 single months and further into weeks. Reverse engineering the goals for 90 days, work on the targets for each week that lead to the monthly target and eventually the 90 days. When you go beyond a 90-day vision, your goals seem far away, so by adopting this principle, it brings everything in close. Whether that be your business strategy, accounts, marketing, sales, employee appraisals etc., everything can fit into this and you will gain more out of using this.

Short-term focus allows you to keep your eyes on the prize with your long-term vision. You can make clearer focused results based forecasts from each 90-day cycle, which will do wonders for being result driven. This will give your business the focus it needs to hit your targets and exceed them.

Together Everyone Achieves More

It's no secret; it takes a team to properly scale a business. Look at Walmart (2.1 million employees) or McDonalds (1.5 million employees). They may be big companies, but remember they started with one person and that's all it takes. You don't want to build a business that just has you in the business alone. That's called the Self-Employment Trap and you've essentially created your own job. As a business owner, that means you own a business, something that should work without you and the first steps to making that happen is hiring people. Create a team.

So far you've learnt about creating your marketing strategy, how to attract more leads and prospects, and converting them into clients. Initially, if it's just you, then you have to do all of these tasks, but once you're at the point where you've got a steady flow of leads, you need to hire a salesperson. You're probably think you don't need more sales, but rather to deliver the services or products you already sold. Whilst that may be true, you still need fresh clients regularly, otherwise the Self Employment Trap will keep you at the manager and technician stage (discussed earlier).

The key to scaling will be consistent sales coming through, which bring in consistent cash-flow. From this place, you can hire the extra help because you haven't neglected sales. Most business owners have neglected this and simply hired help (operations), not sales.

So with that said, how do you go about hiring salespeople? Good question.

When it comes to salespeople, you want top producers. People who eat and breathe sales. They are not average, are not shy, and are not loners. How do you attract top producers? With the very same process discussed earlier about your target audience. Understand what their desires are and make them an offer they can't refuse.

A top producer who sells at these levels is a ***highly influential person*** with ***high dominance***. Two traits that come from a behavioural methodology and tool called DISC. Understanding personality profiling will help you find the right people. Contrary to popular belief, whilst these two traits may seem negatively ego filled they actually aren't. Someone who is highly influential generally has great bonding skills. They connect with people easily and are very likeable. The highly dominant side comes with a never quit trait, meaning after20 rejections they won't give up. They won't quit until all avenues have been exhausted. That's the kind of person who you need on your sales team, Top Producers.

To attract them, your job posting has to be inspiring, and challenging and your sales process must be at another level to what you're accustomed to. With this approach, you can easily set your sights on doubling your growth and more. A great book by Chet Holmes, *The Ultimate Sales Machine*, explores this entire process in great detail and it's what I use in my own business. Get access to some great free tools and download the free resources by visiting www.moreleadmoreclientsbook.com/resources.

I've hired many people over the years and when it comes to salespeople, it's is important they are compensated handsomely. You may ask why should you pay someone else when you can get all of the sales commission? It's simple, remember Wal-Mart? They didn't do it by the owner being at the checkout scanning products and then packing the customers shopping bags. No. You are building a business.

If you have two salespeople that replace you in the selling process, can you see how you're buying back for yourself?

To figure out how much you can afford, start by working out the most you could pay someone for selling your services. The more high value, the better.

For example. If you sell a £5000 service or product, with a 50% profit margin, this means you have £2500 to work with as profit. If you are able to pay a salesperson £1000 (20%) of the sale generated, this leaves you with £1500 profit. If that salesperson generates 10 sales a month (£50,000 total) they earn £10,000. That's £600,000a year for your business and £120,000 a year in commissions for your salesperson. Not bad at all! Can you imagine the types of superstars who would apply for a job paying that much per year? *Top Producers.*

How To Create Your Very Own Time Machine

Since the release of the book,*4 Hour Work Week*, outsourcing and sub-contracting have become a big phenomenon. Tim Ferris ushered in a very technical industry to the general masses and it opened up the possibilities of the laptop lifestyle, or as he calls it "lifestyle design."

If you're new to outsourcing, it's simply the act of hiring somebody (individual or company) outside of your company (immediate team) to perform services or deliver goods that traditionally would have been done in-house. Usually at a reduced cost compared to paying an in-house employee or high rates for experts in a given area where you need assistance. Outsourcing not only gets you the right people at a competitive rate, it allows you to buy back your time.

When you hire people to perform the £10 and £100 an hour tasks, as discussed in chapter 5, you're leveraging time and creating a business that works without you. It's like you're creating your own time machine.

Each hire helps you buy back time, and they run the systems so you don't have to.

There are a number of outsourcing companies for you to be able to hire both individuals and companies. They allow you to post the service/job you need with associated requirements. You can hire the right people through a number of options: hourly rate, fixed project budget, success ratio with past jobs, country, location, language – including fluency level of communication (speaking, written etc), whether they have worked in the past few months, whether they're new or have already earned money, by the skills they list on their profiles and many more options. This makes for a great place to put a job out and hire from anywhere in the world. I've had great successes locally in the UK, USA, Europe and Asia.

The key in the hiring process and ending up with a good outsourcer is to be clear in your job description, check each shortlisted person's profile, and look at past reviews from other employers who have hired them. Read the comments, ask the outsource candidate to submit examples of their past work, set up interviews on Skype and get the answers to the questions you have before you hire. When you have the person or company you wish to hire, depending on the website you use to hire on, they allow you to either set a max number of hours an outsourcer can accrue or you can establish milestone payments on fixed price projects. This is great way to manage your budget and ensure the person will deliver what you need in accordance with the timeline and delivery you have established with them.

The type of people you can hire is wide-ranging but here are a few examples;

- Admin / Virtual Assistant (VA) – Can pretty much do everything with your business:
    - Marketing VA, Social Media VA, Website Management VA, General Client Relationship VA, Public Relations VA, Event Organiser VA, Monthly Reports VA, Customer Service VA, Research VA, Admin VA, Data Entry VA

- Personal Assistant (PA) - An assistant who helps with time and daily management, scheduling of meetings, correspondence, and note-taking. The role of a personal assistant can be varied, such as answering phone calls, taking notes, scheduling meetings, emailing, texts, etc.
- Copywriter – This may be specific for direct response marketing, sales, letters, email campaigns, blogs, PR, etc.
- Web developer – Someone with the expertise to programme and customise websites with knowledge of coding pages and databases.
- Graphic/web design – A worker who understands design and can produce high-level designs for your website and online banners etc.
- Podcast editors – They will have experience of editing episode audio, creating show notes, understand how to upload your media files and submit the episodes to the main podcast marketplaces like iTunes.
- Marketing – A professional campaign manager and/or someone to manage your Facebook Ads and Google Ads campaigns.

By now you're probably starting to see that any area of weakness or low resource in your business can now be outsourced with all the qualifications and experience you require and at a competitive rate. You need a team to truly grow, and now you can do this faster and better than ever before.

To download some of my past job descriptions to use on your own projects visit: www.moreleadsmoreclientsbook.com/resources

CHAPTER ACTION SUMMARY

What you need to put into Action

- Build a team get everyone in the right seats.
    - Get the top performers who align with the values and character traits you wish to have in your team
- Invest in a mentor, coach or advisor who stands by your side and offers expert insight into the best practices
- Base don their experience and own results
- Focus on having great cash flow in your business
- Have long term plans in-line with your vision, while you work the day by day, week by week short terms goals
- Outsource where you can leverage skills and lower costs …

Refer to the MLMC Workbook to work on these key points.
www.moreleadsmoreclientsbook.com/resources

RAISE YOUR AWARENESS OF YOURSELF
WHY YOU SHOULD PAY ATTENTION
EXCUSE
EXCUSE
EXCUSE
EXCUSE
EXCUSE
EXCUSE
ATTENTION
HANDLING TOUGH TIMES,
DESPAIR, DEPRESSION AND STRESS
YOU ONLY HAVE ONE PLACE TO LIVE
BREAKTHROUGH TO SUCCESS
YOU'RE RESPONSIBLE FOR ALL DECISIONS - GOOD AND BAD.
YOU NEED TO HOLD BOTH SHORT AND LONG-TERM VISIONS SIMULTANEOUSLY.
FEELING UNCOMFORTABLE IS YOUR NEW 'COMFORT ZONE.'
YOU DON'T THINK YOU DESERVE IT
YOU DON'T THINK YOU CAN PULL IT OFF
LEARNING IS A CONTINUOUS JOURNEY
NUMBERS DON'T LIE.
LOVE YOUR BUSINESS, BUT BE OBJECTIVE
ENJOY BREAKING RULES
TIME ISN'T LINEAR (SIMPLY TAKE LIFE MOMENT TO MOMENT)
START NOW

Chapter 10

Your Secret Weapon

It took me 28 years before I was even aware and ready to find the answers to the ancient question, "Why am I here?" It's one of those deeper questions we generally tend to ask ourselves. We also question, "When is it going to happen for me? Am I really meant for something bigger than myself?" Whether you've answered this for yourself or not, it all comes down to being aware, looking at your journey and seeking answers to whatever you've found.

Many people don't want to acknowledge this side of their being or simply just don't get what it takes mentally (their awareness level) and personally (their commitment) to be successful. It's also a very none tangible logical driven approach, which makes the logical people run a mile. The goal is to raise your awareness, so you receive a level of understanding of how to make things you see in your dreams and vision happen.

We are all different and have different stories. Some of had a comfortable life, others much tougher. We're all different sizes, shapes, colours, and with different levels of commitment, comfort, which shapes our different desires. So for each of us to be able to reproduce results in our business, the cookie cutter approach may not work time and time again because of these differences.

How does someone who's struggled their whole life with money finally ask to be paid hundreds, thousands or even millions? How does someone who has always worked alone finally build a team to create leverage? And why is it that a person who has lived a comfortable life after finishing school and college cannot even come close to attaining the success they dreamt of, where-as a person who drops out of school and college with a tough backstory goes out and makes a big goal happen?

The answer can be found in awareness and commitment to your goals, beliefs, values, attitude, behaviour, habits, character, strengths and weaknesses (they go hand-in-hand), consistency, no excuse approach and your honesty with yourself (you know... those moments when you're alone with your own thoughts – reflecting back, looking forward and living in the now).

Your success and ability for your business to be a success is not hinged on one thing versus another or improving a weakness in one area or more. It's wrapping the whole thing up and moving forward with all of it, knowing that no matter what, your success is determined by your actions and those actions are either going to propel you, drive you in a different direction or keep you where you are.

We're intricate beings and have many faults. However, we have more great qualities that outweigh the bad and offer us so much more than we ever really give time to consider. There are examples all around us of success in business, personal health and fitness, environment, relationships, family and careers, etc.

Why you should pay attention

The main reason is that **I want you to succeed.** I want you to be honest with yourself. Business or your life is not a place to create excuses around your success. Success is your duty! You're much more than your excuses and it's not easy. It's damn hard, but it's worth it. You've chosen the road less travelled, but it's often the road most rewarded.

This book was not written for you to pick up, learn a few things and move on. It was written because I've helped many coaches and business owners just like you and I know the ideas and concepts shared in this book will make a positive difference to where you go next. It may be one sentence or paragraph that you come across from reading this book, and if that is what you needed to move forward and you took action on it, then I have done my job.

Despair, Depression and Stress

At times, life can feel like a minefield? Where should you focus your energy without feeling guilty that something else needs to be done or completed? The reality is, there are options but before you get to them, you have to go through emotions and different states in order to know who you are.

It might sound a little strange, but until you've failed or gone through some difficulty, how do you truly know what it's like to win. There's a saying that there is no light without the dark and this is true as a business owner. Avoiding temporary failure isn't possible in business and if this is your goal or you're not willing to face your fears, you're setting yourself up for permanent failure. You should probably go get a job, work for someone else and help build their dream.

My first business failed after five years. My cash flow was screwed, my overdraft and credit card limits were maxed out, and I was in a state of panic on the inside whilst trying to maintain an optimistic front on the outside. As I look back, this was a sorry state of affairs. But there's more. Whilst I had a coach, and I was turning over decent money, there was simply too much going out compared to what was coming in and cash gaps in my cash flow were about to cripple my business permanently.

Not only was the business was dying, but I also had team members who I had to let go. It was such a difficult, yet necessary step to take to limit any further worry or financial pain, for both them and me. To this day, it was such a powerful lesson in being able to learn how to take yourself emotionally out of a situation, be objective and lead with integrity.

I felt the pains of failure, the responsibility of my team but ultimately it emphasised the need to not only put into practice the information and concepts I have laid out in this book but to know who I was. To truly be in tune to myself, and not simply being at the mercy of circumstances. Especially the circumstances I created from my inaction and poor decision making.

It was hard, and at the time of my then marriage, it weighed heavy on my relationship, my choices and my options. It made me feel small, inadequate and I seriously questioned myself over the course of years on what I did wrong, who I was, what I thought life was meant to be and how could I change it!

The business had to be liquidated so that I could move on and manage my newly created debts with a clearer approach. I know how that sounds, but honestly, at the time, it was like a breath of fresh air. Whilst I don't envy people going through something like this, it will make you, not break you. Tough times never last, but tough people do (or at least the ones crazy enough to hang in there). I was depressed but had moments of hope and in the end massive action became an instinct to move forward. Action eventually led me out of that place.

I often asked, "What does it take to be successful?"

I realised the process is the same, yet it's different for everyone. Why is it different? Because of the baggage, circumstances, our willpower, strength of character, discipline, determination, and our ability to get back up each time we're knocked down. If they came in the same amounts for everyone, we'd see more successes and probably faster, but the reality is, some people simply want it more than others.

Haters

During your high and low points, there are going to be people who stand against you. People who because they live in a world of lack and negativity, their filter on life is to stand-up against you, like you've become their arch enemy and it's their mission to seek you out or to prove their existence is validated by hating on you. The bottom line is this, when someone judges you, it isn't about you. It's about them and their own insecurities. I see it often, and a lot of the time there's just no logic to it what so ever, so get over it fast and move on. When your reputation is challenged, deal with things swiftly and with a measured approach. Don't post or reply to things with a knee-jerk reply, as this can reflect poorly on you.

The more you grow the bigger your problems become, and this is a good thing. "Get you some haters" – Grant Cardone.

You Only Have One Place To Live

You only have one place to live in this life, so it makes sense to look after your body as best as possible. When you are truly on top and taking care of your health, eating, exercising, emotionally and spiritually, you are in-tune to what is going on around you. A well-oiled engine operates best when it's looked after. Just like a car, it has to have check-ups and be serviced regularly, and when those check-ups are done, your car is more effective and efficient. The same is true of your body.

To maintain optimal performance, take a walk, go for a run, and check how much processed food you eat. Do you actually know what the big food companies put into what you eat? It's no wonder there are so many illnesses.

Imagine putting the wrong fuel into your car; it would go very far, or even start up. So how does that affect you? If you use the wrong fuel and don't take care of your fitness, you'll be less effective, less creative, less productive, lose concentration easily, you'll need more sleep, and the list goes on and on. It will affect your life and business.

I had reminders in my life early on, with losing my father to health issues (which he wasn't even aware of until he died). I don't mention this to panic you. You're in charge and it's up to you. If you know you can do better, then do better. If you're not motivated to take action, then consider for a moment, there's people who depend on you being at your best, and if you're not around for them anymore, you can no longer help.

Breakthrough to Success

There are two key components of belief that coaches must face to break through to success.

1. You don't think you deserve it.
2. You don't think you can pull it off.

To make anything happen, you must believe. With belief, you can fortify the way forward with your mindset. It may not always be the case and your belief and motivation may need topping up, that's okay you're human. As you're committed, that's what counts.

Mindset

Your mindset, the set of attitudes you hold are important to your approach to taking your business to the next level. Consider these 9 points for what will prepare you for moving to the next stage of your journey.

1. You're responsible for all decisions - good and bad.
2. You need to hold both short and long-term visions simultaneously.
3. Feeling uncomfortable is your new "comfort zone."
4. Learning is a continuous journey
5. Numbers don't lie.
6. Love your business, but be objective.
7. Enjoy breaking rules.
8. Time isn't linear (simply take life moment to moment).
9. Start now!

CHAPTER ACTION SUMMARY

What you need to put into Action

- You are the secret weapon, the way through, the goal or dream you desire.
- Work on you, the answer is found in your awareness and commitment to your goals.
- Expect the tough times and difficult emotions that go with this journey - It's part of it.
- There will be haters, but there will also be your cheerleaders - practice being your own biggest fan.
- Take care of home - YOU! Mind, body and soul.
- Push through, break through, flow... You deserve this and you can pull it off, despite the challenges.
- Choose the mind-set of a winner who takes responsibility for all decisions, because you're a winner! …

Refer to the MLMC Workbook to work on these key points.
www.moreleadsmoreclientsbook.com/resources

CONCLUSION

Congratulations! More Leads & Clients

Now that you've read "The 10 Steps of Marketing Success", you've come along way and I'm sure you'll now be able to take these valuable lessons forward with you in your coaching business.

Imagine what it will now be like in your business and life as you implement a marketing strategy to truly grow your business, focus in on your goal, research your market, understand how to carve out your own niche, know their desires, pitch yourself the right way, know the 4P's of your services, understand the level of market awareness and sophistication needed so you can portray the benefits of your USP, and how you will create financial reward that is in-line with your marketing plan. These are lessons most savvy coaches may not have completely grasped before reading this book.

Imagine being able to position yourself as an authority in your niche, and knowing how to wrap your messages into story that will create an identity which allows you to connect deeply with your target audience. Increasing trust and emotionally locking in their desire, taking leads through the process of AIDA, educating them the right way using the EBM formula knowing the exact 5 types of content to create – allowing overwhelm to disappear and certainty to grow.

Envision being able to create the right types of offers that your niche is excited to have, and using headlines that outdo and blow your competition away. Being able to create a systemised marketing asset in the shape of a sales letter that can deliver leads consistently. Knowing that you have coaching programmes and products that excite your target audience with real value to offer. This is a wish and a hope for many coaches – but not you!

Your systems have been created to give you leverage (more time and money), driving fresh new prospects into your business, automatically managing the different levels of where those prospects are in your marketing funnels. Then being able to roll out marketing campaigns on the key media channels that flow into your conversion methods, where you scale risk and increase trust by preparing the best type of prospects as "qualified." You or your sales team predictably convert prospects into clients in a none salesy manner, effortlessly handling objections and on-boarding the most excited new clients.

Your team manages the systems and handle the exceptions, your business is becoming a profitable organisation that is working without you and to top things off, you know how to manage the most important force in your business as you drive it forward – YOU!

Being able to seek guidance from a coach, knowing to dig deep, knowing it wasn't going to be easy, but it would be worth it. You understand what it will take mentally and you're aware that your inner voice on occasion will try to hold you back, but the reality of your situation and your ability to make your vision a reality will only materialise from the action you take and you're prepared for the next level.

This is no longer a pipe dream my friend. Invest your time into work knowing that it will only work if you're in it for the long game, not the short term, because your vision is bigger than any short-term gratification. This is a proven system that you hold in your hands, ready for you to put into action – Now!

This book has been such a meaningful experience. It has sharpened my knowledge around my craft and pushed me mentally, physically and emotionally, because it was time to help those who need it. You, the coaches who make a difference in this world.

Marketing, It's Your Duty!

If an individual or company is better off having worked with you and invested in one of your services because of the results and transformation it can help them to achieve; their life is better for it. You must show up and market your business because the biggest killer of most coaching businesses is obscurity. People don't know you exist. Marketing is the answer.

So, it's with this final thought and the information contained within these pages that I wish you all of the best that this world has to offer. For you to achieve the greatest in reward for the effort that you invest in your business.

Go make it happen!

Leon Streete

A Special Invitation

By now you will have a firm understanding of what it is going to take to strategize, plan, and execute on the key activities to take your coaching business to the next level, but most importantly, making it profitable.

It's been great sharing with you the ideas, concepts, and lessons I've learnt, refined and made throughout my career in marketing for nearly 20 years. I remember being younger and people would make jokes about me, "Where's Leon? With his girlfriend…his computer." It was a backhanded compliment, but what I realize now is that I became obsessed. Obsessed in my pursuit to take an idea and bring it to life. To take my dreams and make them happen. It takes a lot of effort, trial and error and it can also be a slow journey, but I don't like giving up. It takes a special kind of person, usually someone who is too pig-headed to know when to quit. Fortunately, I learnt along the way how to focus and harness this trait to serve me best.

But whilst I acquired this as a new skill in my toolbox of "Go-To Leon Traits," things change, life evolves, new things pop-up and new challenges arise. Wins can appear as if out of no-where and often it can be a case of, how did that happen?

If you're like me, you probably want to speed up the process as best and as fast as possible when it comes to understanding and implementing the valuable content you've learnt.

Even thinking about this stuff can be daunting. How can you fit it all in, even when you're the most enthusiastic and passion filled individual? Well let me put those thoughts to rest and share with you how you can speed up the next steps with you and your business using me as your guide.

The Truth Is... Building a multi-6 or 7 figure coaching business without an "in-the-know" someone who is there to guide you is not easy.

Building a real business is not easy and a successful mentor or coach can sure make it easier. And that's why I'm here to help... I want to show you the easy way, the right way to build it... market it... and set it all up, so you really work less and make more.

There's a new, 100% measurable replacement for old-fashioned business marketing! Imagine how different life would be in you only ever talked to prospects who chased you, those who looked at you as the authority in your market and were eagerly anticipating your product or service.

Do you think you'd feel more successful since you'd be able to finally show people your full potential? That you'd hear people positively talking about you and that life would appear brighter? **This isn't a fantasy**!

If you're serious about building a coaching business that will set you free - both financially and in time - you need to take a careful look at becoming one our exclusive highly valued clients.

There are three ways that I help coaches and depending on where you are in your business; I have a program designed for you.

1. **Elevation.** For established coaches making(£$)250k+
2. **Vortex Mastermind.** For established and growing coaches making(£$)40k -250k
3. **Vortex Plug and Play.** For the start-up and part-time coaches making(£$)20k – 40k

Next Level Help

Let's break down the three options of how you can work with me.

Elevation – Is the only Programme designed to allow coaches at the (£$)250k+ mark to Generate Leads on demand, make sales and live the lifestyle they desire without overwhelm, a poor strategy or technology holding you back.

It's specifically for established coaches already at the mid six-figure mark who are looking to breakthrough to their first million or add another million to what you're already doing. This is an exclusive programme where me and my team work with 30 select coaches each year. It is limited to 30 to ensure the high level of focus and commitment with our clients.

We act as your Strategic Marketing and Implementation Department ensuring we drive your business to the next level of your targets. This is very much a one to one scenario (my company supporting yours) where the emphasis is on strategy and implementation. Because of the high level of service with Elevation, you can only qualify for this service through application and interview only. The reason is that we do not work with just any coach, even if they have the financial resources to invest, is because it's about working with the right client ensuring we have a "win-win" situation.

- Apply for Elevation here: leonstreete.com/elevationapply

Vortex Mastermind – Is the only Programme designed to allow coaches and consultants stuck under the (£$)250k mark, to generate leads on demand, make sales and finally live the £100k+ lifestyle without overwhelm or technology holding you back.

Specifically if you're looking to move beyond low five or six figures, it's essentially an inclusive community with a "Marketing Department In-A Box" approach to coaching you with an implementation stage over an twelve week period for rapid marketing campaign setup – readying you with the steps to scale your business up for the remainder of the year. The Vortex Programme comes with a number of done-for-you features including a fully featured Client-Getting-System (marketing funnel and email marketing automation setup).

Along with this, we meet once each quarter face to face for a two day workshop (three times in the UK and once in the USA), and you receive monthly group coaching calls for a directed approach to executing your marketing plan and then one-to-one calls to ensure you receive the extra support to get you ready to market your business. This programme is limited to 30 people every 12 months and is a gateway to building a well-established multi 6 figure business.

- Apply for Vortex Mastermind here: leonstreete.com/vortexapply

Vortex Plug and Play;

Vortex Plug & Play – Is the only Programme designed to allow coaches stuck under the (£$)40k mark to access the essential marketing system that gives them the insight into the knowledge and processes needed to scale past 40k onto your first 6 figures...

- Get access now:
  www. leonstreete.com/vortexpp

About Leon Streete

Leon Streete is known as "The Lead Generation Coach" and is an advocate for helping Coaches truly succeed in marketing. He is an award-winning podcast host, achieving the honour as, "UK's Best Business Podcast" after interviewing over 100 successful entrepreneurs and experts including Grant Cardone, Bob Burg, Tom Hopkins and Dee Blick.

As an experienced conference speaker, Leon has shared the stage with many leading thinkers and innovators, as well as delivered training and workshops in the USA and Europe.

Leon is also the founder of Business Owner Elevation and creator of the Breakthrough program – ELEVATION "The only Marketing System in the world that allows coaches (business, life, executive, leadership, career, property and relationship) to generate leads on demand, make sales and live "the lifestyle" they desire without overwhelm, a poor marketing strategy or technology holding them back.

Recognized as a thought leader in business marketing and lead generation, you will regularly see and hear interviews on many different podcasts where Leon shares unique ideas, concepts and strategies to help listeners become even more successful.

An important part of Leon's calling is to help those in charitable need and he regularly raises money for young entrepreneurs facing difficult challenges, so they are not limited by their environment or difficult circumstances. To help with donations, please visit www.leonstreete.com/charity

Leon lives in the city of Wolverhampton in the UK.

Receive free resources on Marketing and Lead Generation, at www.LeonStreete.com

Book Leon Streete As A Speaker For Your Event

To communicate with Leon directly about his availability for speaking engagements, speeches, seminars or corporate training programs, consultancy, availability of mastermind meetings, podcast interviews or co-authorship – on the topics of "Marketing, Lead Generation and Business".

Please visit leonstreete.com/speaker
email info@leonstreete.com or phone (+44) 1902-213326

Resources, Scripts, and Tools

To ensure you get the most out of this information, I have created a special resources page that includes:

- A workbook that acts as a guide for the key areas you need to take action onto move your business to the next level using the "10 Steps Of Marketing Success."
- You will also have access to relevant interviews with top experts from my podcast that will help to fortify some of the lessons you've learnt.
- There are also a number of templates and documents I'm sure you'll be able to use instantly in your business that will be very useful.

Visit: www.moreleadsmoreclientsbook.com/resources

Printed in Poland
by Amazon Fulfillment
Poland Sp. z o.o., Wrocław